FERRARI

Stories from Those Who Lived the Legend

JOHN LAMM

BOOK DESIGN BY CHUCK QUEENER

MOTORBOOKS

Ferrari

Dedication

To Lisa and Christopher...thanks for the terrific grandchildren.

From Chuck Queener—art director of this book—and me to our old friend Phil Hill.

First published in 2007 by Motorbooks, an imprint of MBI Publishing Company, Galtier Plaza, Suite 200, 380 Jackson Street, St. Paul, MN 55101 USA
Copyright © 2007 by John Lamm

The information in this book is true and complete to the best of our knowledge. All recommendations are made without any guarantee on the part of the author or Publisher, who also disclaim any liability incurred in connection with the use of this data or specific details.

This publication has not been prepared, approved, or licensed by Ferrari S.p.A., Scuderia Ferrari, or Fiat S.p.A.

We recognize, further, that some words, model names, and designations mentioned herein are the property of the trademark holder. We use them for identification purposes only. This is not an official publication.

Motorbooks titles are also available at discounts in bulk quantity for industrial or sales-promotional use. For details write to Special Sales Manager at MBI Publishing Company, Galtier Plaza, Suite 200, 380 Jackson Street, St. Paul, MN 55101 USA.
ISBN-13: 978-0-7603-2833-0

Editor: Darwin Holmstrom
Designer: Chuck Queener
Cover designer: Kou Lor

Library of Congress Cataloging-in-Publication Data

Lamm, John.
    Ferrari : stories from those who lived the legend / by John Lamm.
        p. cm.
    Includes index.
    ISBN-13: 978-0-7603-2833-0 (hardbound w/ jacket)
    1. Ferrari automobile--History. 2. Automobile engineers-Interviews. 3. Automobile racing drivers--Interviews. I. Title.
    TL215.F47L37 2007
    629.222'2--dc22

                                        2007028856

On the cover: Powering out of a turn, the 599 demonstrates its substantial torque and predictable handling.

On the frontispiece: The Ferrari Enzo, one of the most powerful automobiles ever produced.

On the title pages: The Ferrari F430, the spiritual successor to the original mid-engine Dino.

On the back cover, main: The Ferrari 275 GTB is often considered one of the most beautiful automobiles ever built. Inset: One cannot think about modern Ferrari Formula One racing without thinking of Michael Schumacher. With a record seven Formula One driver's championships under his belt—five earned behind the wheel of Ferraris—Schumacher is statistically the greatest racing driver in history. Of course, he had a little help from the awe-inspiring cars built by Scuderia Ferrari.

Printed in China

Contents

Acknowledgments

FIRST THANKS GO TO ALL THOSE WHO

were kind enough to be interviewed for this book. They were as helpful as they were courteous.

This book couldn't have happened without the encouragement and patience of those at *Road & Track,* especially Editor-In-Chief, Thos L. Bryant; Design Director, Richard Baron; Deputy Editor, Matt Delorenzo; and Senior Technical Editor, Patrick Hong.

At Ferrari, thanks to Antonio Ghini, Dario Benuzzi, Davide Kluzer and Toscan Bennett.

To Brenda Vernor for assistance with interviews in Modena.

Many thanks to those who were responsible for providing Ferraris to be photographed, were helpful in getting the photos done and/or providing wise counsel. In alphabetical order: Bill Baker, Pierre Bardinon, Scott Bergan, Charles Betz, Bob Bodine, Luigi Chinetti Jr., Harley Cluxton, Miles Collier, Ed Davies, Butch Dennison, Robert Dusak, Jeffrey Ehoodin, Joe Galdi, Scott George, John Giordano, Jim Hall, Preston Henn, Marshall Labow, David Letterman, Mitch Leland, Pete Lovely, Bruce McCaw, Anthony Nobles, Paul Pappalardo, Fred Peters, Mark Reinwald, Brian Ross, Peter Sachs, David Seibert, Michael Sheehan, Francois Sicard, Murray Smith, George Stauffer (for the Cobra Daytona Coupe), Thomas Stegmann, Engelbert Stieger, David Sydorick, Steve Tillack, James Truitt, Rob Walton, Tony Wang, Chuck Wegner, Tom Wheatcroft, Sherman Wolf, Lorenzo Zambrano, Eric Zausner, Bill Ziering and our late Ferrari friends, Greg Garrison and Gil Nickel.

My old pal Chuck Queener not only provided the art direction for this book, but also added his knowledge of Ferraris, his collection of brochures and quite a few of the photos. Our wives, Scheri and Beth, provided their unending patience.

Thanks too for the help from MBI, our editor, Darwin Holmstrom, and Zack Miller.

PHOTO CREDITS

I had the pleasure of taking the majority of photos in this book, several while working on-staff for *Road & Track*, which has allowed their use here. I would like to acknowledge the photo work of those listed below. Not mentioned specifically are the anonymous photographers who did the Ferrari, Pininfarina and Italdesign press photos included in this book. Many thanks to them and to:

Enzo Ferrari by Henry Wolf: page 8
Group photo courtesy Ferrari S.p.A.: page 15
Denise McCluggage, by Jennifer O'Sullivan: page 16
Olivier Gendebien by Charles W. Queener: page 16
Courtesy *Road & Track*: page 49
Louis Klemantaski/The Klemantaski Collection: pages 69 and 70
Dan Gurney by Bob Tronolone: page 72
Dan Gurney from the Alexis Callier Collection: page 73
Dan Gurney, Courtesy Edgar Motorsport Archive: page 73

Mike Hawthorn by Bernard Cahier: pages 74/75
German GP by Studio Wörner courtesy *Road & Track*: pages 80/81
Paul Frère from Alexis Callier Collection: page 93
330 TRI/LM courtesy Charles W. Queener: page 96
Le Mans 1964 by Henry N. Manney III: page 111
John Surtees/330 P2 by Studio Wörner courtesy *Road & Track*: page 114
Can-Am Ferrari by Steven J. Earle: page 125
Phil Hill at the Nürburgring 1961 by Studio Wörner courtesy *Road & Track*: pages 128/129
Phil Hill at Reims 1961 by Studio Wörner courtesy *Road & Track*: pages 130/131
Phil Hill at Zandvoort by Bernard Cahier: page 132
Phil Hill and Vittorio Jano by Peter Coltrin courtesy The Klemantaski Collection: page 133
Phil Hill at Zandvoort by Bernard Cahier: page 134
Phil Hill at Spa by Studio Wörner courtesy *Road & Track*: page 135
Phil Hill at Spa by Marcel Ostyn from the Alexis Callier Collection: page 136
Monza by Bernard Cahier: page 137
John Surtees in the 275 P by Studio Wörner courtesy *Road & Track*: page 140
John Surtees by Hal Crocker: page 140
John Surtees at Solitude by Studio Wörner courtesy *Road & Track*: page 141
Giulio Borsari and John Surtees by Henry N. Manney III: page 141
John Morton etc. by Charles W. Queener: pages 152 and 153
Ralph Lauren courtesy Polo: 160
Sam Posey by Charles W. Queener: page 166
Brian Redman by Hal Crocker: page 170
Brian Redman in 312 PB courtesy Motor Trend: pages 170 and 171
Jacky Ickx by A.B. Shuman courtesy *Motor Trend*: page 174
Mario Andretti at Questor GP by John Lamm courtesy *Motor Trend*: page 182
Mario Andretti and Mauro Forghieri by John Lamm courtesy *Motor Trend*: page 183
Mario Andretti by John Lamm courtesy *Motor Trend*: pages 184 and 185
Dario Franchitti courtesy Acura: page 198
Mauro Forghieri by A.B. Shuman courtesy *Motor Trend*: page 206
Luigi Chinetti by Charles W. Queener: page 231
Blur shot by Paul-Henri Cahier: pages 232/233
Eddie Irvine etc by Paul-Henri Cahier: pages 234/235
Monaco pit wall by Charles W. Queener: page 236
Luca di Montezemolo by Paul-Henri Cahier: page 236
Michael Schumacher by Paul-Henri Cahier: page 237
Ferrari factory photos courtesy Ferrari S.p.A.: pages 240, 241 and 242
Ferrari Challenge by Richard Prince courtesy Ferrari North America: pages 244 and 245
Michael Schumacher in the rain by Paul-Henri Cahier: pages 278 and 279
Victory by Paul-Henri Cahier: page 281
Courtesy Anthony Nobles: page 283
Ferrari factory photos courtesy Ferrari S.p.A.: page 285
Brochure scans courtesy of Allied PreMedia Solutions, Branford, Connecticut.

Introduction

Let's start this book with a joke.

It's a funny little story in which President Ronald Reagan is visiting the Pope. Reagan notices that His Holiness has a golden telephone next to him. He asks about it and the Pope gives him a knowing nod, points toward Heaven and smiles.

Reagan says, "Really, I'd love to make a call."

"You're welcome to," says the Pope, "but it costs 35 million lira, in cash."

Taken aback, Reagan can only say, "Gee, we don't carry that kind of cash with us."

"Sorry, it's out of my hands," explains the Pope.

The very next day, Reagan is meeting with Enzo Ferrari in his office at the Fiorano test track when he notices Ferrari also has a golden telephone. He points to it and comments, "I see you have one of those. Too bad it's so expensive. I'd love to make a call… you know where."

"Expensive?" asks an amazed Enzo Ferrari. "It's only 50 lira."

"But," Regan inquires, "why is it 35 million lira from the Vatican but only 50 lira from Maranello?"

Ferrari smiles and explains, "From here it's a local call…"

Try telling that same story but substitute the name of other great automotive leaders—Henry Ford, Ettore Bugatti, Soichiro Honda, Colin Chapman—and it isn't particularly funny.

Why? Despite all the genius in the works of these other automotive greats, there simply isn't the Italian soul and spirit in their automobiles that is found in Ferraris. Engineering genius, artistry, value, power, and speed can be experienced in various Bugattis, Hondas, Lotuses, and Fords, but not that something special that makes Ferraris look so good in a strong, passionate red.

Ever recall anyone wanting to be buried in a Ford, Bugatti, Honda, or Lotus? Didn't think so. But in the late 1970s, anyone who read the Los Angeles Times learned about Sandra West, a Beverly Hills woman who requested that she be buried, dressed in a gown, behind the wheel of her 1964 Ferrari. Her wish was granted.

In doing a Ferrari book, the biggest obstacle is other Ferrari books. There are shelves of them, from general histories to highly detailed studies of individual models or series, like the 250 GTOs, the Testa Rossas, or the Formula 1 cars. And they are printed in a grand variety of languages.

Enzo Ferrari photographed by Henry Wolf

Don't even think of Googling the word "Ferrari" on the Internet unless you have plenty of time on your hands.

So why do another?

Two reasons. One is that no one seems to tire of looking at Ferraris. That goes right back to the emotion and passion. The visual power of a 357 Plus race car, the styling of the Superfast 1 show car, the stance of a Berlinetta Boxer, the wonderfully outrageous shape of the Formula 1-inspired Enzo… these are always worthy of another look.

Second, after more than 30 years of covering Ferrari, the one thing that sticks with me even more than the historical facts are the personal stories that go with them. Phil Hill describing the year he won the Formula 1 championship for Ferrari. Mario Andretti explaining how he dealt with Enzo Ferrari. World Driving Champion John Surtees on quitting the Ferrari team during the Grand Prix season. Carroll Shelby reminiscing about Ford trying to beat Ferrari. And Sam Posey talking us through a hot lap of Le Mans in a 512 M.

In this book, stories such as these are brought to life in one-latte or one-cabernet doses to enjoy, one sitting at a time.

One last thing before you immerse yourself into the following pages. There are, in a sense, two Ferraris. The first is Enzo's Ferrari, the company founded just after World War II. Rebuilt from bomb damage, the company worked hard to get its first cars on the road, then to make Ferrari the most famous and best known race-winning automobiles in the world.

Ferrari's death in August 1988 coincided with a time of amazing growth and strength in the exotic automobile business. Within a few years, however, that began to fade and the business got tougher. This was also the period when great technical strides were being made and Ferrari needed a new leader.

Enter Luca di Montezemolo, who led Ferrari's resurgence in Formula 1 in the 1970s and has helped transform Ferrari from its traditional corporate self into an industrial power-house. He oversaw the F1 team's growth into a period of dominance and helped turn the

Maranello factory into an industrial showplace. Montezemolo has since become the chairman of Fiat Auto.

This change at Ferrari began in 1991 and mirrors a similar changing of the guard at another specialist automaker: Porsche. The German firm was bleeding money in the early 1990s before Wendelin Weideking took over and developed Boxsters, Cayennes, and new 911s, making the company profitable again.

It's all a matter of knowing how to transform an automaker with a grand tradition and a deep well of good feeling into a modern, profitable company. It's a trick that Ferrari has managed with skill, and one that a few other well-known car companies haven't seemed to master.

And with that, enjoy. F

Ferrari Formula 1 team manager Luca di Montezemolo (left) with Fiat Chairman Giovanni Agnelli at the 1975 Monaco Grand Prix.

Enzo Ferrari

WITH THE REVERENCE MOST PEOPLE

reserve for the Sistine Chapel, the Louvre, or the Smithsonian, we gazed around the courtyard at Fiorano.

We were, after all, car guys, so being at Ferrari's test track, where all the company's race and production cars are developed, was fascinating.

This was 1978 and Fiorano had only been finished six years before, but it was already part of Ferrari lore. There's a 1.85-mile race circuit, with telemetry to track cars through every corner, and the restored farmhouse that now contained offices.

Most important, over there, behind a red door, was Enzo Ferrari's office. Wonder if he's in today?

On cue, Franco Gozzi, Ferrari's right-hand man, steps out of the door and declares, "Ah, the Americans. You cannot visit the Vatican without meeting the Pope." And with that he ushers us into Ferrari's office for a half-hour audience with The Man. We discussed the state of racing and Ferrari told us he considered the three most important races to be the Monaco Grand Prix, the 24 Hours of Le Mans, and the Indianapolis 500. Having already won the first two, it was his hope to one day win at Indy.

We felt honored to be there, and in Catholic Italy, Gozzi's analogy to the Papacy didn't seem out of line. At that point, Enzo Ferrari was 80 years old and easily the closest thing to royalty in the automobile business, an honor he'd earned over decades.

For a man whose name is so well known throughout the world, Enzo Ferrari never strayed far from home. Born February 18 (but apparently registered on the 20th), 1898, in Modena, he grew up in a comfortable home. His father, Alfredo, owned a successful metal fabrication shop.

Reportedly Alfredo had one of the first automobiles in the area and when Enzo was 10 he took the young man to a race in nearby Bologna. The impression seems to have stuck.

Both Alfredo and his eldest son, also Alfredo, died of illnesses in 1916, possibly in an early round of the pandemic that killed millions around the world in the half decade before 1920. Enzo, now in the Italian army, also became quite ill and was mustered out at age 20.

After trying several jobs, he moved to Milan and ended up working with the company that built CNM automobiles. They gave him his first shot at driving a race car in a hillclimb near Parma.

This led to a seat on the Alfa Romeo team and Ferrari got off to a good start, finishing second in 1920 in the difficult Targa Florio in Sicily.

Ferrari began to move to the development and testing side of the team, though he continued to race. The win that gets the most attention was in Ravenna in 1923 when the parents of Francesco Baracca were so impressed they gave Ferrari a piece of the fabric from the aircraft in which their son died during World War I. On it was the family's prancing horse emblem, which Ferrari used on his team's race cars beginning in 1932 and is now the most famous automotive symbol in the world.

In early 1929, Alfa outsourced its racing efforts from the factory to newly formed Scuderia Ferrari in Modena. Enzo Ferrari's race driving had been trailing off for years and he quit completely in 1932 when his son, Alfredo (nicknamed Dino), was born.

Ferrari was busy enough building a strong racing organization at 11 Viale Trento Trieste in Modena. At its core were the men who would one day form the heart of his development team when Ferrari became an automaker.

Luigi Bazzi joined Alfa Romeo in 1923, went to Scuderia Ferrari when it was formed, and remained Enzo Ferrari's lead development engineer until his retirement in the early 1960s. Bazzi would be the technical soul of Ferrari for decades.

Vittorio Jano was the genius who designed many of the great Alfa Romeos for Scuderia Ferrari. Jano went to Lancia after World War II but returned to Ferrari when it inherited the Lancia race team and its Jano-designed D50 Grand Prix cars in 1955. The engineer then penned the famous line of Ferrari V-6 Dino engines.

Gioacchino Colombo, a protégé of Jano, created the famous Alfa Romeo two-stage supercharged 158/159 Alfetta Grand Prix engine for Scuderia Ferrari. After World War II he designed the first Ferrari V-12, which was the basis for thousands of venerated engines.

Alberto Massimino worked on the Alfetta engine and was instrumental in the design of Ferrari's only prewar cars, the Auto Avio Costruzioni 815s.

In 1938, Alfa Romeo decided to take its race team back to Milan and retained Ferrari as manager, but the following year differences between Ferrari and Alfa management caused a permanent split. Ferrari returned to Modena and, under the terms of the breakup, couldn't build a car with his name on it for four years.

This is why the first two cars built by Ferrari were called Auto Avio Costruzioni 815s. Built for the 1940 Mille Miglia, this duo had 1.5-liter 8-cylinder engines created by mating pairs of Fiat engines. Wrapped in pretty bodies by Carrozzeria Touring, the 815s were the quickest of the 1.5-liter class, though neither finished the race. One 815 survives.

All this became unimportant with the outbreak of World War II. Ferrari did war work and moved his factory a 10-mile drive south to the village of Maranello, away from the bombing threat in a city center. Still, the factory was bombed twice.

On September 16, 1946, the first Ferrari V-12 was fired up, and that's where the history you will find in the following pages begins.

As you go through them, keep this in mind: We know Ferrari today as a successful, highly profitable industrial superpower, but it wasn't always that way. Enzo Ferrari had his financial struggles, highs and lows, race wins, and days of sadness in those years when racing was so deadly.

His son Dino passed away in 1956, though it turned out he had a second son from a liaison with Lina Lardi. Born in 1945, Piero Lardi-Ferrari was publicly acknowledged in 1978 after the death of Enzo Ferrari's wife, Laura. Piero Ferrari is now Vice Chairman of Ferrari and owns 10 percent of the firm, Fiat having 90 percent.

Through it all, Enzo Ferrari persevered and remained the preeminent voice in the

Dott. Franco Gozzi

Enzo Ferrari's divorce terms from Alfa Romeo prohibited him from building a car bearing his name for four years. So when commissioned to create two cars for the 1940 Mille Miglia, Ferrari built them under the name Auto Avio Costruzioni and called them 815 for their Fiat-based 1.5-liter 8-cylinder engines. Carrozzeria Touring bodied the roadsters, which led their class in the 1000-mile race until sidelined by mechanical problems. One 815 still exists and is used on vintage events.

To commemorate the popular Canadian Grand Prix driver Gilles Villeneuve, who was killed in practice for the 1982 Belgian Grand Prix, this bust was erected outside Ferrari's Fiorano test track.

Enzo Ferrari (left) and Sergio Scaglietti talk about one of the Alfa Romeos entered in the historic Mille Miglia during the rally's stop in Modena. Scaglietti became the major car body builder for Ferrari and eventually sold his firm to the automaker.

company, even after retirement.

Today, when you talk with people who worked closely with Enzo Ferrari, they all quickly tell how honored they were to have worked for the man and the company.

They are just as willing to tell you Ferrari could be a tough guy.

Franco Gozzi was to Enzo Ferrari what Mario Andretti calls, "the right hand of the father." Gozzi had various official titles, but he was, in fact, Ferrari's closest advisor.

Gozzi says Enzo Ferrari "was a fantastic man," but adds that he was, "a demanding master." Continues Gozzi: "If he expected 130 percent from you, the first time you worked 125 percent he started complaining. He was never satisfied, a slave driver." In his next breath, however, Gozzi calls Ferrari "wonderful" and adds, "He couldn't have made Ferrari without being this way.

"We are very few in number, but everybody who worked with Ferrari is proud because I think everybody has the feeling they participated in a big adventure. It was a privilege to be a part of the fantastic Ferrari.

"He was a very intelligent man… and he was lucky. I remember a few times when he was

really lucky, but this is the way of every big man, and you aren't lucky for 70 years."

Gozzi explains another side of Ferrari when he speaks of Gilles Villeneuve, the popular Canadian driver for the team who was quick, spectacular, and very popular, but who died in a Ferrari during practice for the 1982 Belgian Grand Prix:

"When a driver, your driver, your man is killed, well, I cannot say Ferrari was used to this, but he didn't demonstrate emotion."

And yet, adds Gozzi, "When we wrote a page in memory of Gilles, he wanted me to put at the end, 'I loved him.'"

Gozzi finishes: "I asked one time why he was so cold," and Ferrari told him, "My teacher, Antonio Ascari (a great race driver and father of the equally famous Alberto), told me that he didn't show any sentiment with his wife and his son because he didn't want them to feel so badly when he was gone."

Sergio Scaglietti built the bodies of many famous Ferraris, owning the shop favored by the company. Eventually he sold his firm to Ferrari and the bodies of many of Maranello's cars have been created in the traditional Scaglietti factory on the Via Emilia in Modena.

Scaglietti had a close working relationship with Enzo Ferrari and in Ferrari's later years they had lunch together every Saturday.

The 87-year-old Scaglietti grins and explains, "He was a very hard man to work for because if you asked for 10 he'd give you 8," but continues, "I had a passion to do something for him."

He says that when Ferrari arrived at his shops with his hat back on his head you didn't want to talk with him because he was in a bad mood.

Still smiling, Scaglietti explains that Ferrari, "was very stubborn, and working with him could be like going to the cinema, to a drama."

And yet to Scaglietti, "Ferrari was a super man. He couldn't be a normal person.

"Ferrari knew about everything and everybody. When he had 200 journalists in front of him he replied to every single one. They'd ask a question and he gave them the answer immediately, no matter the subject. He was phenomenal, very intelligent."

Denise McCluggage, one of the United States' most accomplished woman race drivers in the 1950s and 1960s, often raced Ferraris. For decades since, McCluggage has been one of the more entertaining and insightful automotive writers in the country, male or female. She knew Enzo Ferrari and many of the people who were a part of the great man's life.

"Enzo Ferrari wanted to be any of three things: a sportswriter, a tenor or a race driver. He

At the meeting described by Mario Andretti, Enzo Ferrari greeted many of the drivers who had raced Ferraris. From the left: Cliff Allison, Phil Hill, Giannino Marzotto, Michele Alboreto, Dorino Serafini, Nanni Galli, Andrea de Adamich, Gino Munaron, Umberto Maglioli, Maria Teresa de Filippis (general secretary of the Former Grand Prix Drivers' Association), José Froilán González, Enzo Ferrari, Cesare Perdisa, Piero Taruffi, René Arnoux, Clay Regazzoni, Tino Brambilla, Juan Manuel Fangio, (Mario Andretti is hidden, but next to Fangio), Sergio Mantovani, Maurice Trintignant, Luigi Chinetti, David Piper, John Surtees, Olivier Gendebien, Innes Ireland, Patrick Tambay, and Gerhard Berger.

Paul Frère   *Olivier Gendebien*

Denise McCluggage

had no voice, so he couldn't be a tenor. He was a good writer—he wrote his own books. And he was a moderate racing car driver."

And yet ironically, she explains, "What he did best was to be a tenor because he had the perfect temperament of a tenor. Extremely romantic and overly emotional. It was all an act in a way, though it was very sincere at the moment.

"His great love for his son, Dino, was only recognized after Dino was dead, because there was great drama in that. The bereaved father spent more time at his son's grave than he actually did with Dino.

"He was furious with Louise King Collins because she had stolen Peter (one of the famous British drivers on the Ferrari team) away from spending every day at the factory and constantly being there and, in effect, being Ferrari's son. But after Peter died (racing a Ferrari) Louise went to see Ferrari at his behest. He was all weepy and said he never went to races anymore, but he would go to Monza with Louise.

"And as wedding present he had given them a beautiful Ferrari.

"So he was back and forth, extremely emotional."

McCluggage explains her take on what would now be called Ferrari's management style: "He liked to keep things on a light fire, to keep the popcorn popping. Some people can use tension well. There are certain baseball managers for whom that works because that tension is on a high wire and if it's a highwire act it's good. But if it isn't a highwire act, something a little more plodding, it doesn't work.

"Ferrari was unsuccessful some years because it didn't work. The year after Phil's Formula 1 championship (Phil Hill in 1961), for instance, the car was dreadful because perhaps some of the tension had been released by the championship. And then, of course, Chiti and the others (team manager Carlo Chiti and several important engineers) went off and did other things, perhaps because of the tension.

"Sometimes the release of tension can be more detrimental than the tension itself, and tension is difficult to apportion properly. But when it works, it works extremely well. And Ferrari was excellent at that."

McCluggage then adds, "Pearls can't be created without a bit of sand, an irritant. Raindrops don't fall without a nucleus of dust, so there's some part of a pure thing that is impure or it wouldn't exist at all. It wouldn't be created. Ferrari was that irritant.

"He couldn't do much himself, but he could get other people to do great things."

Among those who raced for the Maranello team, Mario Andretti had a closer than usual relationship with Enzo Ferrari. Says Andretti: "The most important part was the fact I could deal with him directly. And that was not a given. Talk with many of the drivers who drove for Ferrari and some had a direct relationship, but most didn't. They had to speak with the right hand of the father—Dr. Gozzi—or some other liaison, because Mr. Ferrari never wanted to be put on the spot.

"For some reason, we used to exchange telegrams directly and if I was asked to drive, he would call me. If there was anything I needed, any discussions, I would talk with him, so that in itself was something very special.

"Honestly, I expected that, but it wasn't a given and I realized that more and more. Ask Carlos Reutemann. I think he talked to the old man maybe twice in all the times he drove for Ferrari.

"When I was called back to substitute for Pironi in 1982 at Monza (regular Ferrari driver Didier Pironi had suffered a brutal accident during practice for the German Grand Prix), I had been out of Formula 1 for a year and had never driven one of the 1.5-liter turbocharged race cars, which were like a bombshell. So I went in a week ahead and we tested at Fiorano."

Ferrari's famous test track has cameras aimed at every segment of the track and a driver's progress can be followed by way of a bank of monitors. Enzo Ferrari kept an eye on the test session by Andretti, who explains, "He was there all day and they said he had never done that. I put 87 laps in that day and he came back with a smile on his face because I set a lap record toward the end of the day.

"That's all you really wanted to get from him. If you got a smile out of him, it was huge, because you never got too much reaction. That was a sign of approval."

The 42-year-old Andretti put the turbo Ferrari on the pole at Monza to the joy of the *tifosi*, as the fervent Ferrari fans are called in Italy. "And he was there. Monza was the only place he would go, but it was so satisfying."

In 1987, to celebrate the 40th anniversary of the first race win by a Ferrari, drivers who had competed in Ferraris in major races were invited to Maranello. The celebration involved several days of watching vintage Ferraris racing at the nearby Imola race circuit, the inevitable long lunches and dinners, plus one very special meeting.

Before we get to that meeting, it's important to appreciate that most race drivers live in the here and now, without much appreciation of the good old days. Get the newest equipment, shave away hundredths of a second in lap times, win races. No time for sentiment.

So it seems ironic that Andretti and Phil Hill, the only two U.S. drivers who have won the Formula 1 World Championship, are sentimentalists with a strong sense of their sport's history.

Andretti recalls that special meeting in Maranello: "Mr. Ferrari invited all the living drivers who had raced for him. To me it was a glorious day in so many ways, just looking around at the individuals I drew inspiration from, drivers like José Froilán Gonzáles and Maurice Trintignant, people like that. I didn't even know they were still alive.

"These are guys I admired greatly, guys from the era when I fell in love with the sport. I knew this was a moment in my life that will never be repeated, an incredible event."

After one lunch in Maranello at the Cavallino restaurant across from the factory, the drivers were asked to go to the racing department. A Ferrari public relations man, Pietro Defranchi, motioned for two journalists—Jeff Hutchinson and me—to come along. We couldn't write about what we were going to see now, he explained, but maybe sometime in the future.

In a small room were all the drivers: Juan Manuel Fangio, Phil Hill, Tony Brooks, Olivier Gendebien, Paul Frère, Maurice Trintignant... the list goes on and on and, of course, included Andretti.

When everyone was seated, 89-year-old Enzo Ferrari was escorted into the room and began to say goodbye to his drivers. It was a highly emotional meeting.

Andretti remembers it well:

"First of all, he clearly gave absolute credit to the drivers for Ferrari being what it is today. He said, 'It's because of you, because of what you've risked, because of what you have created for us that we are what we are.'

"That was emotional enough.

"We were like a classroom with pupils from different eras and he was the big master up front, the professor. To be honest with you, I don't know if you can use the proper adjectives from where I sat to describe that.

"That weekend was the last time I saw him. He was such a stern individual person, and always in control of a situation. I'd been at a number of press conferences where he was in total control, and this was the first time I saw emotion in his face. I thought it must be very special for him as well.

"It was a momentous day for all of us."

Enzo Ferrari died August 14, 1988. ▣

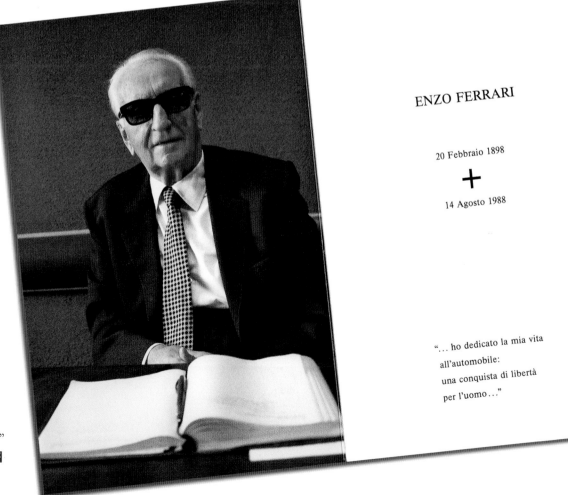

ENZO FERRARI

20 Febbraio 1898

✝

14 Agosto 1988

"... ho dedicato la mia vita all'automobile: una conquista di libertà per l'uomo..."

The 1940s

Ferrari in the 1940s

THE DEATH OF ENZO FERRARI MARKED

the end of the first Ferrari era, which essentially began with rebuilding the factory after World War II and Ferrari being able to build his own cars.

It's been said Enzo Ferrari was enamored with the V-12 engines of Packard, so when he needed his own powerplant he had Gioacchino Colombo design one. The first V-12 ran in September 1946, by which time Colombo had already returned to Alfa Romeo.

Development continued, thanks to Luigi Bazzi, and on March 12, 1947, the first Ferrari automobile—actually a chassis without a body—was driven from the factory by Enzo Ferrari. Come May 11, Ferrari was ready for a race in the city of Piacenza, an event Franco Cortese led in the Ferrari until a fuel pump broke.

Giancarlo Radighieri started working at Maranello in 1945 at age 14 and continued through Enzo Ferrari's tenure at the factory. He remembers the company employees going to that first race—as a prize for doing all they could to help get the car ready—and they weren't riding in the luxury buses used today.

It was actually a truck, and it was fitted with seats from the factory's canteen, long benches on which people could sit close to each other. The folks from Ferrari left for Piacenza early in the morning and it took them three hours to get to the track because they could go only 25 mph.

"It was the first race and we were very proud to be a part of the car," Radighieri explains. "And we brought plenty of food and Lambrusco [the well-known local wine]."

Previous pages: Phil Hill in the 1949 Le Mans-winning Barchetta.
Built by the Ferrari factory, the automobile at the right is a replica of its first car, a 125 Sport. With Franco Cortese driving, the V-12-powered car dropped out of its first race with technical troubles, but won the second time out, May 25, 1947—Ferrari's first race win as an automaker. Above is the cover of a very rare first-generation Ferrari sales brochure.

Two weeks later, Cortese scored Ferrari's first win in Rome driving a car called the 125. As with Ferrari V-12s, for many years the name came from the displacement of one cylinder. Twelve times 125 equals 1.5 liters, but the engine needed to race in the 2.0-liter class, so by August the engine was opened up to 1902cc at 159 per cylinder, hence the type 159 engine. This was followed shortly by the famous 166, whose V-12 displaced 1995cc, even closer to 2.0 liters.

Paul Frère, a Belgian motoring journalist and a winner of Le Mans for Ferrari in 1960, remembers his first visit to Ferrari in 1948. Frère recalls that even though the factory was in Maranello, "the main office was still in Viale Trento Trieste in Modena and there was also a Ferrari workshop there with cars being built."

At the time, "There weren't many cars on the roads and many of those roads were dirt, not asphalt. Virtually the only cars you saw on the roads were Fiats.

"There was a lot of enthusiasm for the car at Ferrari. Modena was famous for its artisans and there were many workshops around town. If you needed a gear tomorrow morning you could order it the evening before and you would have it."

Many of the Ferraris built throughout the 1940s were meant to race, some as sports cars, such as the initial 125 or the classic Touring-bodied Barchettas.

Others were the Spider Corsas, cigar-shaped machines with cycle fenders. Frère recalls, "Ferrari personally explained the car, telling me the 2.0-liter car could be used as a sports car or as a Formula 2 car just by removing the lights and fenders. He was quite nice and open."

Some of what most people would think of as "street" Ferraris with normal production car amenities began to appear with bodies by Stablimenti Farina and Touring.

And for Grand Prix racing, the 125 version of the V-12 was supercharged to a reported 230 horsepower.

There were any number of variations on these themes to fit the changing rules as racing sorted out its classes after World War II. Most important to Enzo Ferrari and his need to establish credibility were race victories. Cortese's place at the top of the Ferrari winner's honor roll was followed by others with victories in the rugged Mille Miglia in 1948 and 1949, and on the very fast Spa circuit in Belgium.

The most important race, however, came in 1949 when Luigi Chinetti and Lord Selsdon

Well-known sportsman Briggs Cunningham bought the first Ferrari to be raced in the U.S., a cycle-fendered Spider Corsa bearing serial number 016-I (above). Below is one of the most important race cars in Ferrari history, the 166 Barchetta driven by Luigi Chinetti and, in a much lesser role, Lord Selsdon, to win the 1949 24 Hours of Le Mans, a landmark for Maranello.

The oldest Ferrari in existence is the cigar-shaped 166 Corsa Spider (above) with the serial number 002C, here driven by Ferrari World Champion Phil Hill. These early Ferraris could be raced in sports car events or, fenders removed, as formula cars. At the right is 002C's functional dashboard.

Tommy Lee of Los Angeles bought the first Ferrari Barchetta (below) when it made its debut at the 1948 Turin Auto Show. This was also the first Ferrari delivered in the U.S. and is an excellent example of Touring's trademark Superleggera (super light) designs, which paid great attention to not only weight, but also aerodynamics. Note the grille in this Barchetta is not the typical eggcrate design seen in most Ferraris of the era.

won the 24 Hours of Le Mans in a 166 Barchetta. Chinetti drove more than 23 hours of that race and the Ferrari proved to be as much a tenacious bulldog as the driver.

In one of the world's most important automobile races—easily the best-known European event in the important U.S. market—a Ferrari automobile proved to be as reliable as it was fast. And it didn't hurt that the 166 was dressed in Carlo Felice Bianchi Anderloni's Barchetta bodywork by Touring, which had one of the prettiest and most important automotive shapes in the second half of the 20th century.

Ferrari was ready for the next step. ◨

Carlo Felice Bianchi Anderloni (left) gets credit for the landmark design of the Ferrari Barchetta. The simple lines work not only on the open Barchetta but also on a coupe, such as the 1949 166 MM Berlinetta below.

The 1950s

*Ferrari's 1952
sales brochure.*

*Previous pages: Despite a crumpled fender
and the use of only 4th gear, Gigi Villoresi
won the 1951 Mille Miglia in this Ferrari
340 America Vignale coupe. One of his
main competitors was Giannino Marzotto
in the strange Reggiani-bodied Ferrari 212
seen below.*

The 1950s

PRODUCTION CARS
From one-offs to series production

HAVING PROVEN THE WORTH OF GIOACCHINO COLOMBO'S V-12 ON THE RACE
track, Ferrari started the 1950s with a new engine.

One of Enzo Ferrari's goals was to beat his former employer, Alfa Romeo, in open-wheel
racing. That would be tough, as Alfa had the powerful 159 Alfetta Grand Prix car with its
Colombo-designed supercharged 1.5-liter straight-8. Rules allowed a non-supercharged
alternative up to 4.5 liters, and that formula's champion at Ferrari was Colombo's replacement
in Maranello, Aurelio Lampredi. Informally, Colombo's Ferrari engines are known as the
"small-block" V-12s and were made in displacements from 1.5 to 4.4 liters. Lampredi's "big-
block" V-12s ranged from 3.0 liters up to 4.9.

1950 166 S by Touring

1951 340 America by Vignale

1951 212 Export by Ghia

1951 225 S by Vignale

1951 212 Export by Vignale

1952 212 Export by Vignale

Throughout the 1950s, street Ferraris were built with both types of powerplants, though halfway through the decade Colombo's design began to dominate and, with refinements by other engineers, was used in Ferraris for decades.

During roughly that same period, Ferraris meant for the public roads were made as one-offs or in very small series. Originally the coachbuilding firm of Touring had much of the business of designing Ferrari bodies, and then Vignale took over for a period. Carrozzeria Ghia got its hand in for a time, as did Stabilimenti Farina, Boano, and a man who would become very important in coming years, Sergio Scaglietti.

Increasingly, however, Ferrari design was being taken up by Pinin

Sales brochure for the 1953 212 Inter lists all the race victories from 1947 through 1952.

Ferrari [**29**

This rather amazing-looking machine is a Vignale-bodied 1952 Ferrari 340 Mexico with a 4.1-liter Lampredi V-12. In 1952, Gigi Villoresi raced the car in the Carrera Panamericana from Guatemala through Mexico to the U.S. border. In the colors seen here, Phil Hill and Richie Ginther competed in Mexico with it in 1953, eventually crashing.

1951 212 Export by Vignale

Farina (which became Pininfarina in 1961). The first true series production Ferrari was the 1954 250 GT Europa with a 3.0-liter version of Colombo's V-12.

There were still special-bodied Ferraris being created and most of these were also penned by Pinin Farina, often on longer 410 SA (Super America) chassis with the 4.9-liter Lampredi V-12. Many of us would argue that the greatest of all was Pinin Farina's finned Superfast 1 shown at the 1956 Paris auto show, followed by a limited series of big, fin-less 410 coupes and a few spiders.

Come 1959, Ferrari production really hit its stride with the handsome (if not spine-tingling) 250 GT. This design is best seen as the open cabriolet version.

The change of emphasis from special-bodied cars at the opening of the decade to series production cars 10 years later was setting the scene for Ferrari in the 1960s. ⧅

Sales brochure for the 1956 Pinin Farina designed 410 Superamerica. The graphics for many of the catalogues were created by the great Italian painter Antonio de Guisti.

1952 340 Mexico Spider by Vignale

1953 735 Mondial by Pinin Farina

1953 250 Mille Miglia by Vignale

1953 340 America by Vignale

1954 250 GT Europa by Pinin Farina

Aurelio Lampredi's big-block V-12 in a 1953 340 America race car. Fed by a trio of Weber carburetors, the engine had a factory rating of 280 horsepower.

Sales brochure for the 250 Europa and 375 America of 1952 and 1953.

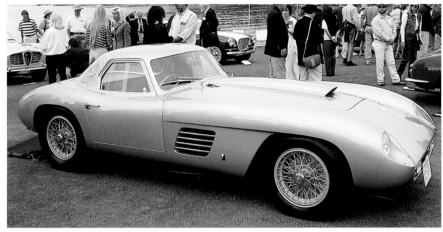

1955 375 Plus by Scaglietti

1955 375 Mille Miglia by Pinin Farina

1956 250 GT by Pinin Farina

1956 250 GT by Boano

1959 250 GT "Interim" by Pinin Farina

Above: The sales brochure for the 250 GT Cabriolet, Coupe and Berlinetta. Left: The Boano Coupe brochure.

Although Zagato was not the favored carrozzeria for Maranello, it built bodies for a number of Ferraris. This is one of five Zagato-bodied Ferraris on the 250 GT long-wheelbase chassis. Originally built for Vladimiro Galluzzi on chassis number 0515, this athletic shape features Zagato's well-known "double bubble" roofline. The car is now owned by David Sydorick and has been a class winner at the Pebble Beach Concours d'Elegance.

• Robert M. Lee's First Ferrari

Businessman
Reno, Nevada

ROBERT M. LEE HAS A SOFT SPOT FOR FERRARIS, WHICH CERTAINLY ISN'T UNUSUAL. HOWEVER, THE STORY of how he came to own his first is unique.

Lee is now one of the United States' foremost collectors of fine automobiles. One of his cars, a 1931 Daimler Double Six, won Best of Show at the 2006 Pebble Beach Concours d'Elegance. Fifty years ago, however, Lee knew little about cars.

Then he met American race driver Masten Gregory, who had a home in Rome. Lee was passing through Rome on his way to an African safari and they had dinner. Through Gregory he met Ivana Lelli and as he didn't speak Italian, Lee asked Lelli to guide him on what would be his first tour through Italy.

She agreed and a few days later they were in Modena. Lee had heard of Ferrari and asked Lelli if they could visit the now-famous automaker.

Robert M. Lee with Phil Hill.

That is where Lee's half-century story begins, and keep in mind that he was just 18: "We went to the Ferrari garage and she asked the fellow who seemed to be in charge if her American friend could look at the cars. He said yes, but explained these cars are in for service and belong to customers and he's welcome to look at them, but not to touch them.

"My eyes were bugging out. I saw this beautiful silver 250 Europa Pininfarina coupe and that's the one that caught my eye. A few minutes later the fellow, who seemed to be the service manager, came out and said, 'Mr. Ferrari is here from the factory and he would like to meet the American visitor.'

"Wow. Ferrari was already an Italian hero and quite a guy. I met him and he opened the door of the Europa and said—through Ivana—that I should please sit in the car and tell him how it feels.

"Well, I sat in the car and I had to tell him that it feels great but my head hits the roof. Mr. Ferrari laughed and said, 'But Ferrari is a shoemaker. And if Ferrari makes a car for you the roof will be higher.'

"He asked, 'Are you going back to Rome before the weekend?'

"I answered, 'Yes.'

"He told me there is to be a concours d'elegance in a park in Rome and we will be showing our new 250 GT production car. We hope to make about 50 of them. I would like to invite you to try the car.

"I said, 'Mr. Ferrari, thank you for your generosity, but I will never buy one these cars. I'm naturally curious about them because they are so

great, but I don't want to take advantage of your hospitality.'

"He said, 'You have come to visit Ferrari. Ferrari insists that you drive the car.'

"He also said, 'If you ever want to buy a Ferrari you buy it from Ferrari and not from Luigi Chinetti in New York.'

"So I thanked him and he asked where I was staying in Rome. I told him the Excelsior. He said, 'Okay, the car will be at the Excelsior at 10 o'clock on Monday morning. But you should go to the concours d'elegance.'

"I was very excited and thanked him and we went to the concours and saw some magnificent cars. Sergio Pininfarina won an award and I went over and introduced myself, congratulated him, and got to talking with him. I mentioned I visited Ferrari in Modena the other day and that he has invited me to try his new production car. I asked, 'Are they reliable cars?'

"He grinned from ear to ear and said, 'You can never break the engine.' And that was true.

"On Monday morning at 10 o'clock the car appeared and I'm sure the driver was Piero Taruffi (one of Italy's most famous post-war drivers). He drove me out of town into the countryside so I could drive the car. I drove it and it felt like a nervous animal. That was my introduction.

"I went to Africa and later wrote a thank you letter to Ferrari. I shot a rhino on that trip and I had the four feet mounted as humidors, but I had one made for him with a sterling silver cigarette box in the lid and the Ferrari horse engraved by my gun engraver.

"The following Spring I went to the New York Automobile Show and made a beeline for the Ferrari stand. I saw a gentleman in charge of the stand and this beautiful, beautiful car that had been made for the Geneva Show, which was a few weeks before."

This was a now-famous show car on a Ferrari 250 GT chassis with a convertible body by the Italian carrozzeria, Boano.

"I asked the fellow, who turned out to be Luigi Chinetti, the price of the car. He said the car is not for sale. It belongs to the factory and has to go back after the New York Show.

"I went home and sent a long telegram to Ferrari reminding him of my visit and how he told me that if I ever wanted to buy a Ferrari I should buy it from him and not from Luigi

Robert M. Lee has many great Ferraris in his collection (above), one of the most recognizable to fans being this 250 GT (below), which was the 1957 Geneva show car and the prototype for the elegant Series I Spiders. Note the cut-down driver's door. The car's first owner was Ferrari factory team driver Peter Collins, who had Dunlop fit it with disc brakes at a time when Maranello preferred drum brakes.

Robert C. Wilke, whose Leader Card roadsters won the Indianapolis 500 three times, had Ghia build the body for a Ferrari 410 Superamerica chassis. Ghia's famed designer Giovanni Savonuzzi had been creating his "Gilda" designs for Chrysler and that is the shape of Wilke's 412, seen above in Robert M. Lee's collection. Boano did another 410, a coupe version of Lee's 250 Boano on the longer 410 chassis (right). The car's rear window predates the Corvette Sting Ray's split window coupe.

Chinetti. I mentioned I saw this car from Geneva at the New York Show and I would very much like to buy it. I told him I had saved $9,500 from my fly-tying business and I offered that for the car.

"A couple of days later Luigi called me and he said, 'I don't know who you are. I never saw you in my life. But we have this wonderful car from the Geneva Show, which you saw in New York. It has to go back to the factory and I am the exclusive importer of Ferrari for North America and I cannot buy the car. I don't know how you know Mr. Ferrari, but he has told me I must sell you the car for $9,500. It cost the factory more than double that to build. Bring me a cashier's check for $9,500.

"My mother drove me into New York, I paid Luigi for the car and he took us on a demo run. My mother was in the passenger's seat and I sat on the luggage bench in the back. Luigi drove like a mad man. I think he was very upset. He went over to the East River Drive and was driving like a maniac. He came down Park Avenue snaking back and forth.

"That was the beginning and I think Ferrari made a pretty good judgment by giving me a good deal because I've bought a few cars since then."

Lee still owns the Boano show car along with its sister car, a coupe version on a 410 chassis. Lee and the one-owner 250 GT Boano were honored at the 2006 Pebble Beach concours. **F**

Robert M. Lee and Anne Brockinton leave the awards ramp at the 2006 Pebble Beach Concours, where Lee was honored for the 50 years he has owned his Ferrari 250 GT Boano cabriolet.

This Pinin Farina-bodied Berlinetta began life in 1953 as a 4.1-liter 340 MM, but was later made into a 4.5-liter 375. In its race life it was driven by many of the heroes—Mike Hawthorn, Gigi Villoresi, Alberto Ascari, Giuseppe Farina, Umberto Maglioli—in venues from the greenery of France's 24 Hours of Le Mans to the dusty straights of Mexico's Carrera Panamericana.

• Antonio Ghini

Communication and Brand Management Director
Ferrari S.p.A.
Maranello, Italy

ANTONIO GHINI'S MOTHER WARNED HIM, "AH, FERRARI WILL BE A DISASTER FOR YOU."

Well, that "disaster" started for Ghini when he was just 17 years old:

"I was born in Bologna, near Modena, and extremely passionate about sports cars because the Mille Miglia crossed Bologna. Every year I was waiting for the Mille Miglia.

"There was a weekly magazine called *Auto Italiana* that was printed by the same printers who did *Quattroruote* [a famous Italian automotive magazine]. It was a sporting magazine that came every Thursday."

Each Thursday, Ghini got up early so he could read the magazine before he went to school. On one issue's cover was a coupon that offered, "The first 12 people who send this coupon back to *Auto Italiana* will be given a visit to Ferrari."

"Without any hesitation, instead of going to school, I went to the station and took a train to Milan. At 11:30 I arrived at the magazine's offices and asked, 'How may have you received?'

"'Not one,' they said. 'You are the first.'"

Having traveled the 135 miles to Milan, Ghini now had to face the music at home. He telephoned his mother, who was a schoolteacher. "I called at 1 p.m. and said, 'Mama, I can't come home for lunch.'"

"Why?" she asked. "Have you not been to school? Where are you?"

"I am in Milan," admitted Ghini.

"Why?" she asked.

"Because of Ferrari."

At that precise moment his mother uttered those famous words: "Ah, Ferrari will be a disaster for you."

She did not, however, stop her son from collecting his prize. "I went and I still have the picture of my visit," Ghini says with a smile. "I met Enzo Ferrari. We were taken to the Fini restaurant for lunch. It was a great experience."

And it was far from a disaster for Ghini. Years later, he rose to be Ferrari's Director of Communications and Brand Management. **F**

Between 1956 and 1960, Ferrari built 33 410 Superamericas in three series. Powered by 4.9-liter, 380-horsepower Lampredi V-12s, most had dramatic Pinin Farina bodywork. The car seen here was built in 1959 and its first owner was casino magnate and Ferrari dealer Bill Harrah. Bill Rudd ran the dealership service shop and modified Harrah's Ferraris for his tall frame. Harrah loved cruising from Reno to Las Vegas and back when Nevada had no speed limit on its open highways.

This is a pair of ex-Bill Harrah Superamericas now owed by Eric Zausner. Next to the green 410 SA is one of the later 400 Superamericas with its Pininfarina (the firm had changed its name from "Pinin Farina" by this time) "aerodinamico" body shape. To accommodate Harrah's love of cruising at high speed on Nevada highways, Bill Rudd upped the 4.9's horsepower from 340 to 360. The 400's 4.0-liter Colombo-based V-12 was opened up to 4.6 liters and bumped to 420 horsepower.

• **Chris Cord on the 410 Superfast**
Retired
Ketchum, Idaho

WHEN ERNIE MCAFEE WAS KILLED RACING A FERRARI 121 LM AT PEBBLE BEACH, HIS MENTOR AND FRIEND, William Doheny, changed his plans. Doheny's stepson, Chris Cord, explains, "He had a 3.5-liter Monza on order to replace the 121 LM and after Ernie's death he said that's enough racing for me. The Monza was already paid for so Mr. Ferrari said, 'I have a very beautiful Superfast in the Paris Auto Show. How would you like that?'" Doheny figured, "Why not?"

Cord remembers: "The Superfast was a beautifully finished car with the leather and the black crackle dash. It had a 4-speed transmission with synchromesh, which shifted beautifully. The only thing a bit problematical was that it had a high first gear. You were forever slipping the clutch to get it off the line trying to get that heavy beast going, so you were changing clutches every 5000 miles."

Cord describes the dream of any young Ferrari fan: "I can remember one time when Steve Earle took his 300 SL and I had the Superfast and we raced all the way up the mountains on the back roads to Lake Arrowhead from west Los Angeles. That Ferrari absolutely flew. It had the most beautiful howl from the V-12 and the exhaust note. It was something pretty special.

"It drew a lot of attention wherever you went with it. People's jaws would drop and ask what it was and chat for hours… it is one of the prettiest cars ever designed."

Reality comes home when Cord describes the handling: "Trucky, with a very heavy brake pedal and heavy steering—typical of Ferrari of that era. But with lots of horsepower, which is where the development was… just put a bigger engine in. It was a 5.0-liter V-12 with three 2-barrel carburetors, but for normal driving it was fine except for that long first gear.

"My dad took that car on a couple of Turismo Visitadores [an informal and legendary group of drivers who once tore through the Nevada desert at high speed]. I wasn't a part of that, but they headed across Nevada and he said they were running 170 mph. The fastest I ever saw in the car was about 130 until I ran out of straightaway and had to stop the thing... and you had to begin your stopping early and use both feet on the pedal.

"Dad had Ernie McAfee Engineering up on Sunset Boulevard and the car was forever in there with Tom Bamford. They must have changed clutches two or three times. Then he said the heck with it and he sold it to (actor) Jackie Cooper."

After Cooper the Superfast owner list includes a short honor roll of well known Ferrari enthusiasts: Peter Sachs, Greg Garrison, and now Robert M. Lee. **F**

♣ **"My dad took the car on a couple of** *Turismo Visitadores.* **I wasn't a part of that, but they headed across Nevada and he said they were running 170 mph."**— *Chris Cord*

• Sergio Pininfarina
Honorary Chairman, Pininfarina
Torino, Italy

"No one ever choked swallowing their pride."
ANONYMOUS

FERRARI AND PININFARINA HAVE BEEN SYNOMOUS FOR DECADES. IN THE EARLY YEARS, FERRARIS WERE wrapped in bodywork from various carrozzeria, including Vignale, Touring, and Ghia. Come the mid-1950s, however, those name plaques affixed to the bodywork of Ferraris disappeared in favor of designs from Battista Pinin Farina.

The first Pinin Farina-bodied Ferrari body came in 1952, a cabriolet built on a 212 chassis, a handsome, elegant machine now in the collection of Robert M. Lee in Reno, Nevada, an old friend of the design firm.

It made sense in the early 1950s that Enzo Ferrari and Battista Pinin Farina would work together, as both were already Italian legends: Ferrari for his Alfa Romeo racing years and his growing car company. Pinin Farina for the bodywork his firm had designed and built for chassis from such famed automakers as Lancia, Fiat, Alfa Romeo, and even Cadillac.

But there was a problem: pride, apparently in equal parts.

Trying to bridge that gap was a new engineering graduate, Sergio Pininfarina (we slip into the modern spelling here, as the family name was changed from Pinin Farina to Pininfarina in 1961).

Bringing the two important men together was tough duty for a 25-year-old just spreading his wings within the family business. Relaxing at the Paris Auto Show 55 years later, Sergio Pininfarina can smile and tell the tale:

"I was quite young. I had gotten my degree in 1950 and spent a few months abroad, so I was really in the first months of work, but I was the man chosen by my father to create this contact with Ferrari. New man, young engineer, young friendship.

"I tried to organize a meeting between Mr. Ferrari and my father. They were two strong personalities and they wanted to meet and to become friends and cooperate, but my father was a proud man, as was Mr. Ferrari. Neither of the two wanted to make the first step, not Mr. Ferrari to say, 'I go to Torino,' or my father to say, 'I go to Maranello.'

"Every time I tried to organize such a meeting my father would say,

'Oh, I would like very much to meet him. Why doesn't he come to see us in Torino?' This was impossible."

Seen through 21st century eyes, with Ferrari the best-known automotive name in the world, it seems odd that anyone would question meeting with the automaker to conduct business. But times were different then. Great automobiles for the wealthy were custom-designed one-off cars from coachbuilders on individual chassis from specialist firms like Ferrari or Maserati. Series production of exotic cars was still over the horizon, but far-seeing men like Sergio Pininfarina knew the world was changing. How could the young engineer bring Ferrari and his father together?

"I succeeded in arranging a meeting halfway," he explains. "It was 1951 and the meeting was in Tortona, a small town approximately halfway between Torino and Modena. I say Modena and not Maranello because at that time Ferrari was in Modena.

"I remember we met in a restaurant and had lunch and immediately the two great men had a great sympathy and feeling for each other. They both wished to start this cooperation. Ferrari had admired the work of my father. My father had the feeling Ferrari was a new, young firm that would become representative of the Italian industry, especially in the sporting field. So the ambiance was right and everything went well… and I am lucky to say I was present at the very beginning of my career at the historical meeting."

Was the young Pininfarina nervous? "No, not nervous, but the commitment was heavy and important for me and for my career and my firm. I was feeling all the weight of the responsibility and put 100 percent of my commitment into it. Fortunately, after the first difficult days, Mr. Ferrari started to like me, this young man full of enthusiasm, and he developed a favorable attitude."

Like many of the men who admired Enzo Ferrari, he also admits, "Mr. Ferrari was a difficult character. My father too sometimes had some sharp angles and could be difficult, [but Ferrari] had sympathy for me. First, he was a severe judge, then a friendly judge, and then he was just a friend. I had tremendous respect for Mr. Ferrari and his attitude toward design.

"Mr. Ferrari could understand if a man was being sincere and he understood my enthusiasm was sincere and coming from the heart."

How deep was the friendship between Ferrari and Pininfarina?

"In 1966 my father died and Mr. Ferrari, who rarely went out of Modena, came to Torino by car. On that occasion he told me just one thing: From this moment on we call each other by name, Sergio and Enzo. In Italian life to call each other by your first names is important because it is a step from formalization to a sentimental, human relation.

"At that moment it was the best thing Ferrari could tell me. I was very impressed and very happy. This reinforced our relationship."

Years later, Sergio Pininfarina was offered the presidency of the federation of all Italian industry and declined, despite a request from Umberto Agnelli of the powerful family that owns Fiat.

"In February 1988, Mr. Ferrari was turning 90 years old and some days before his birthday I left Torino in my car with my three children to take an album of drawings that were specially made on that occasion for him. It was the best gift I could give to show him how happy I had been to work with Ferrari.

"I entered the room with my three children, Lorenza, Andrea, and Paolo. Mr. Ferrari was not very well, and I remember that when he saw Lorenza entering he sat up straighter—it is a method of education; an old gentleman sees a young lady and he shows a sign of respect. This moved me.

"I was trying to give him the gift, and I put my heart in it, but before he looked at what it was he said, 'Sergio, you must go to Rome,' which meant that I had to accept to be nominated president of the Italian industry. 'Sergio, you must go to Rome because I want you and you are the right man.'

"I was so proud and so moved that I finally accepted."

Sergio Pininfarina, the young engineer who managed to bring Enzo Ferrari and Battista Pinin Farina together, went on to serve on numerous committees not just in Italy but also in the European community and has a long list of honors for design and public service. In 2006, his 80th year, he assumed the position of Honorary Chairman at Pininfarina when his son, Andrea, became Chairman and CEO. ☐

✦ *"I tried to organize a* **meeting between Mr. Ferrari and my father. Neither of the two wanted to make the first step, not Mr. Ferrari to say 'I go to Torino,' or my father to say, 'I go to Maranello."**
— *Sergio Pininfarina*

This 1958 sales brochure for the conservative 250 GT Coupe gives Pininfarina great prominence on its cover.

Pinin Farina built this handsome cabriolet, his first body for Ferrari, on a 212 Inter chassis in 1952. Originally sold to Georges Filipinetti, the Swiss Ferrari importer, it was eventually bought by U.S. collector Robert M. Lee, a friend of Sergio Pininfarina. Lee had the Italian carrozzeria restore the car and it was delivered back to Lee on Enzo Ferrari's 90th birthday.

Sports Racing Cars

GRAND TOURING AND SPORTS RACING CARS
Barchettas, Monzas, and Testa Rossas

Previous pages: Two Le Mans-winning Ferraris driven by Phil Hill and Olivier Gendebien, the 1958 250 Testa Rossa in the foreground and the 1962 330 TRI/LM. Above: The 4.5-liter 375 MM with its exciting Vignale body in which Phil Hill and Richie Ginther competed in the 1954 Carrera Panamericana. For years this car was hidden away from prying eyes.

RACING FERRARIS BEGAN THE 1950S IN GRAND STYLE WHEN GIANNINO MARZOTTO won the Mille Miglia in April in a closed Touring-bodied 195 Ferrari.

As with production Ferraris, the first half of the 1950s saw the company racing cars with both the Colombo and Lampredi V-12s. It was often a "horses for courses" situation with the small V-12 cars suited to the shorter, tighter tracks, and the big-engine cars to the longer, faster circuits like Le Mans.

Then a funny thing happened mid-decade.

Almost from the beginning of his time at Ferrari, Aurelio Lampredi had argued they needed 4-cylinder engines, which had an advantage not in horsepower, but torque, that measure of twisting power from low revs that is very handy on tight race tracks.

Lampredi did two designs of the four, one called Mondial, the other, which was a bit larger, labeled Monza. The Mondial proved a success in the 2.0-liter class, which was important in Europe.

There were several variations on the 4-cylinder theme, and by mid-decade the larger four had been developed into the 3.0-liter 750 Monza as the 3.0-liter 250 V-12 faded in importance. The four would be developed into the 3.5-liter 857 and 860 Monzas, which the factory team used in international competition. And in 1956 the team had to use the 2.5-liter 625 LM at Le Mans.

This move to inline engines made sense when you consider Mercedes-Benz's success with its straight-8 SLRs and Maserati's strong inline-6. Lampredi's next move was a straight-6, ultimately resulting in the 121 LM, an impressively powerful car that Phil Hill thinks got a bad rap because it was never fully developed.

By 1956, Enzo Ferrari had tired of the 4- and 6-cylinder experiments. The small displacement fours would continue to be quite successful in the 2.0-liter category, fitted in one of the most beautiful Ferrari race cars of the era, the 500 TRC. But for the big classes the factory cars returned to the latest development of the Colombo V-12, and the fours and V-12s—the 860 Monza and 290 MM—raced concurrently in 1956.

By mid-decade Lampredi was gone and after a few big-horsepower 410 race cars in 1955, so was his V-12 from competition.

continued on page 66

1955 121 LM by Scaglietti

1954 375 Plus by Pinin Farina

1957 500 TRC by Scaglietti

1955 410 Sport by Scaglietti

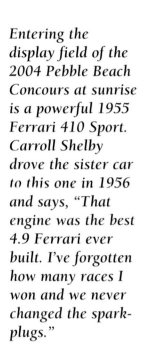

Entering the
display field of the
2004 Pebble Beach
Concours at sunrise
is a powerful 1955
Ferrari 410 Sport.
Carroll Shelby
drove the sister car
to this one in 1956
and says, "That
engine was the best
4.9 Ferrari ever
built. I've forgotten
how many races I
won and we never
changed the spark-
plugs."

For 1954, Ferrari increased the size of the Lampredi V-12 from 4.5 liters to 4.9 liters and mounted the engine in the 330-horse-power 375 Plus. Pinin Farina shaped the body for this 375 Plus, and an identical car driven by José Froilán Gonzáles and Maurice Trintignant won the 1954 24 Hours of Le Mans. While the 375 MM had a live rear axle, the Plus used a De Dion layout. This suspension system forced Pinin Farina to create the lump on the rear deck to clear the spare wheel. This 375 Plus is from the collection of Ralph Lauren.

Ferrari printed this 8 3/8 x 6-inch card (left) showing a beautiful 375 Mille Miglia spider by Pinin Farina but called it a 410 Superamerica. Looks like he's driving it to the office doesn't it?

• Gino Munaron on the 750 Monza
Race driver, retired
Valenza, Italy

The Ferrari 750 Monza above is important in U.S. road racing history. Phil Hill won the Del Monte Trophy at the Pebble Beach races in 1955 with this car, while Carroll Shelby won the event the following year in the car. Jim Hall of Chaparral fame now owns the Ferrari.

GINO MUNARON RACED FERRARIS IN THE 1950S AND WAS PART OF THE FACTORY team in 1957 and 1958. He recalls how the 750 Monza could be a treacherous race car, saying this was likely because while Aurelio Lampredi may have been a brilliant engine designer, he was not that talented at developing a chassis. He says Lampredi didn't even get a driver's license until after he'd left Ferrari.

In France, the 3.0-liter, 4-cylinder Monzas were known as *la tueuse*, or "the killer."

Munaron just avoided being a victim himself at France's Montlhéry circuit. For 40 laps the Monza he was driving had been perfectly capable of a making a corner that involved the car flying through the air for 20 feet off a jump. Munaron then had to be hard on the brakes and downshift, downshifting two gears before turning right.

On the 41st lap, however, he landed, nailed the pedal, and only the left front brake worked. The Ferrari snapped sideways and began to flip, eventually sliding upside down for hundreds of feet, Munaron's helmet grinding on the pavement. (The helmet is now in Ferrari's museum in Maranello.)

When the car stopped, the driver could feel gasoline dripping on him and knew he had to get out of the overturned Monza quickly. This meant grabbing the hot exhaust pipe to haul himself out, but it was easily the lesser of many evils.

Out from under the Ferrari, Munaron rolled away from the wreckage and managed to stand up. Bloodied and with a broken shoulder and sternum, he was collecting his wits when a French official ran up and asked him, "Is there anything you need?"

Stunned by the stupid simplicity of the question, Munaron quipped, "Yes, an aperitif." **F**

Gino Munaron was a Ferrari factory team driver in 1957 and 1958. Below is the Aurelio Lampredi-designed 3.0-liter 4-cylinder engine used in Ferrari's 750 Monza.

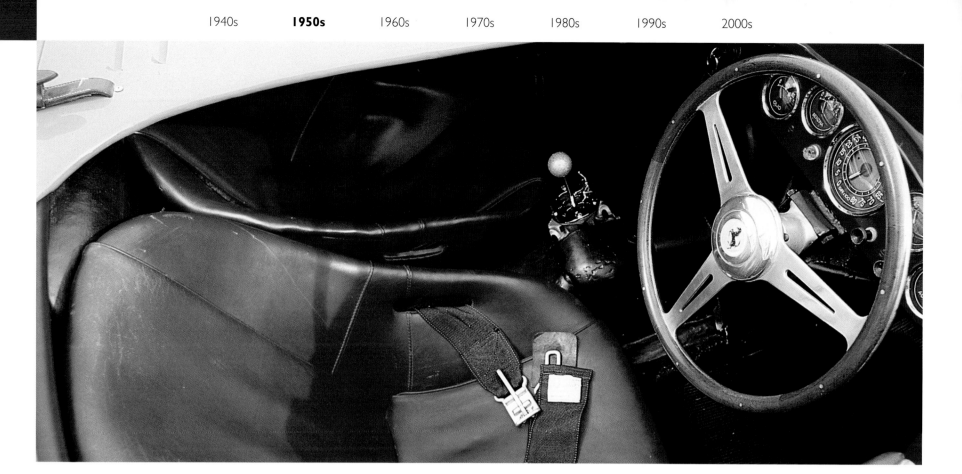

• Chris Cord on the 121 LM
Retired
Ketchum, Idaho

BEFORE CHRIS CORD WENT ON TO BECOME THE 1987 IMSA CAMEL GT DRIVER'S CHAMPION IN A TOYOTA Celica for Dan Gurney's All-American Racers, he'd raced a powerful Chevrolet Monza GT. But what lit his modern competitive fires was an old Ferrari with a family history.

Cord's stepfather, William Doheny, was an early proponent of Ferrari in Southern California and had entered a 121 LM powered by a 4.4-liter straight-6 in the main event of 1956 Pebble Beach road races. Driven by the talented Ernie McAfee, it would be a frontrunner, but McAfee crashed the Ferrari into one of the stout trees that lined the track. He was killed and road racing disappeared from Pebble Beach.

"Ernie McAfee had this magical, wonderful smile," Cord tells us. "He was a warm, friendly, enthusiastic man… very easygoing and a complete gentleman. Just talking to him you'd never know he was a race driver or a super mechanic, but just a regular guy.

"He was also a good driver and very close to my father. When Ernie was killed I think my father was in a state of depression for at least a year. We could barely speak to him he was so upset by the whole thing. It was awful to see."

✤ **"The 121 was a car I had enormous respect for,** *but you wanted to make sure it was pointed in the right direction before you stood on it . . . it wasn't a car you hustled along."* — *Chris Cord*

The Ferrari 121 was almost cut in half in the wreck and it was sent to a shop and rebuilt over a period of a year or year-and-a-half. "The frame was rewelded and they replaced sections of the body and then my dad threw a cover over it for years. When Steve (Earle) was starting the Monterey Historics (in 1974) I said to my father, "this car would fit perfectly in that kind of a venue, and what do you think about my showing the car and running a few laps?"

"He thought about it for a few days and said go ahead, but be real careful. That allowed me the opportunity to run it." And that's what got Cord back into racing and, eventually, his driver's title.

Looking back to driving the 121, Cord admits, "It was a horrible handling car, nowhere near as nice as a 4-cylinder 750 Monza or 3.5-liter Monza. Very nose heavy because of the weight of the engine and you had to be careful with brake bias. I think that was one of the things that caused Ernie's accident, leaning on the brakes real hard. It would just stand right up on its nose and on that long straight you're kind of going downhill anyway, so that probably exacerbated it.

"The 121 was a car I had enormous respect for, but you wanted to make sure it was pointed in the right direction before you stood on it… it wasn't a car you hustled along. It was very fast, but not a fun car to drive." 🄵

Ernie McAfee was driving this Ferrari 121 LM in the feature race at Pebble Beach in 1956 when he crashed and was killed. These 4.4-liter straight-6 race cars were well known for their speed, but also had a reputation for being a bit brutish.

In 1956, Ferrari was ending his 4-cylinder era and raced both the car on the left, a 3.5-liter 4-cylinder 860 Monza—this car won that year's 12 Hours of Sebring—and the 3.5-liter V-12 290 MM (above and right). Below right is the 860 Monza's predecessor, the 857 Monza, which also has a 3.5-liter inline-4. All these beautiful shapes were created by Sergio Scaglietti.

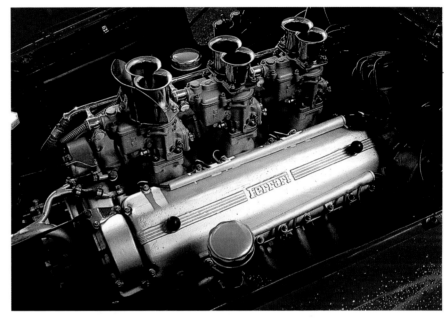

Anticipating the 3.0-liter engine displacement limit for 1958, Ferrari began development of the 250 Testa Rossa in 1957 using the car above. With the devilish serial number 666, it was the first Ferrari with Scaglietti's "pontoon" fenders meant to cool the front brakes. At the right is the 1958 250 Testa Rossa Phil Hill and Olivier Gendebien drove to victory in that year's 24 Hours of Le Mans.

A bird's eye view of the 1958 Testa Rossa. Note the four-spoke steering wheel.

continued from page 52

What followed in 1957 was considered by many Ferrari team drivers to be the finest car the team raced that decade, a beautiful machine with a twin-cam version of the Colombo engine called—as its displacement grew—the 290 Sport (3.4 liters), 315 Sport (3.7 liters) and 335 Sport (4.0 liters). Ferrari put it to good use, winning the World Championship for Sports Cars, adding to its titles from 1953, 1954, and 1956.

Responding to a tragic accident at the 1955 24 Hours of Le Mans, plus rising sports racing car speeds, the rule makers trimmed displacement of the sports racing cars to 3.0 liters as of 1958. This fed right into Ferrari's hands with the single-cam version of the Colombo

Ferrari created the 412 MI "hot rod" (above) with a special V-12 that started life in the 335 S in which Alfonso de Portago was killed in the 1957 Mille Miglia. It was next fitted to a single-seater to compete against Indianapolis roadsters in a race at Monza in Italy. Meant to beat Chevrolet V-8 specials like the Scarabs, the 412 MI had only one major victory. Below is a classic example of a 1959 250 Testa Rossa.

V-12. The resulting Testa Rossas were not only exciting-looking race cars, but won both the 24 Hours of Le Mans and the sports car championship in 1958.

Asked which was the greatest of all Ferrari engines, Paul Frère, the racing writer who co-drove to victory in the 1960 24 Hours of Le Mans and has tested most every car from Maranello for decades, declares, "For me it will always be the 3.0-liter V-12 of the end of the 1950s and early 1960s. It was smooth, flexible, and powerful, developing 100 horsepower per liter, which in those times was quite rare."

There was also a beautiful Ferrari that looked like a 3/4-scale Testa Rossa but powered by the Dino V-6 in 2.0-, 2.4-, and 3.0-liter forms.

We began this section mentioning Ferrari won the 1950 Mille Miglia with a closed car and

should finish it with mention of the company's great Grand Touring race cars of the decade. While they didn't always get the attention of the open sports racers, the GTs put in some remarkable performances.

While a few Vignale-bodied GTs were successful, this was very much a Pinin Farina show, from the 375 MM Berlinettas to the mid-decade 250 GT Tour de France models—named for their success on that tough automotive event—to one of great Ferrari gems of all time, the 1959 short-wheelbase 250 GT Berlinetta or, to any Ferrari fan, simply the SWB. ▣

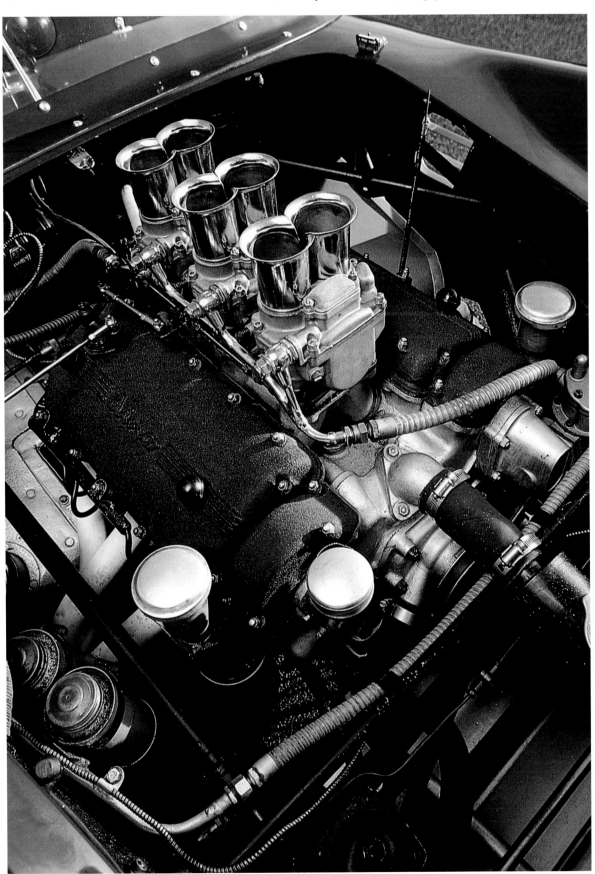

Looking like three-quarter scale Testa Rossas, Dino sports racing cars were raced with V-6 engines displacing 2.0, 2.4, or 3.0 liters. The 2.4 mounted in the 246 S was effective on the twisty Targa Florio circuit in 1960.

• Louis Klemantaski

Photographer
Coombe Hay, Great Britain

WE ALL HAVE AUTOMOBILE RACING HEROES, BUT WHAT ABOUT A RACING PHOTOGRAPHY HERO? NOT just for the many great photos he took, but for being a highly regarded co-driver on that great open road race, Italy's Mille Miglia.

For five years, Louis Klemantaski navigated the 1000-mile race, nonstop from Brescia to Rome and back, telling the

driver what the road ahead would be like... fast, curving, slow... and photographing the view from the second seat with a pair of Leica C3s.

Klemantaski died in 2001 at the age of 89, but in 1996 he competed in the historic Mille Miglia rally with Peter Sachs, the man who now owns the Ferrari 335 S in which Klemantaski competed with fellow Briton Peter Collins. We had the pleasure... no, make that the honor... of spending a morning in Brescia, Italy, before the start of the rally, talking with Klementaski.

He explained that after three years with Aston Martin, he switched to work with his good friend Collins and the Ferrari team on the event in 1956 and again in 1957, the year a tragic accident forever ended the Mille Miglia as a pure racing event.

The 1956 Mille Miglia, "was a wet one," Klemantaski began, "We battled on and went pretty well. Towards the end, on the long

Piacenza straight, we were doing pretty well.

"Some oil fumes began coming up and, of course, coating Peter's and my visors. I would lean over and clean his and the moment it was covered again he'd have to sort of peer underneath the visor. There was nothing dry left in the car. I'd used everything up. . . but we finished second (in 11 hours, 49 minutes, 28 seconds in a Ferrari 860 Monza, just eight minutes behind winner Eugenio Castelotti's Ferrari 290 MM).

In 1957, "I think we were the last of the Ferraris to start, and that car (the 335 S) was different as chalk to cheese compared to the year before, much more power. Peter was delighted. He thought it was absolutely wonderful and it was really thrilling. He said it was the best-handling sport Ferrari he'd ever driven.

"We went very well. Somewhere near Ancona, on a fast winding road we caught up (Count Wolfgang) Von Trips, who had started two minutes ahead of us. I just don't know whether he did it on purpose, but we could

not get past. He was weaving in front.

"Peter was flashing the lights, I was blowing the horn. He took no notice. And then at last I was able to give Peter a signal that the next corner is a rather fast one that doesn't look to be. So Von Trips slowed down slightly and we outbraked him and got past, and then we just went away.

"We were the first in Rome, faster than Stirling Moss Mercedes' time, and were just going ahead. But then Peter wasn't happy taking the right-hand bends, with a noise coming from the back. When we got to the Bologna control, Ferrari, who was there, wanted us to retire. Peter said, 'No, no, we haven't got far to go, we'll just try it.'

"So we went on and it got more and more difficult with more and more noises from the back. Just before entering Parma there was no drive. And at that time we were 11 minutes ahead. It was THE most wonderful drive of Peter's, I must say. . ."

His notes on the 1000 miles got to be so

Opposite page: Louis Klemantaski relived his 1957 Mille Miglia experience with Peter Collins in a Ferrari 335 S when he rode with the current owner of the car, Peter Sachs, in the 1996 version of the Italian road race.

The factory courtyard before departing for Brescia. Left to right, Gino Munaron's 500 TRC, white-haired Piero Taruffi with his back to the camera stands next to his winning 315 S. Olivier Gendebien leans against the 250 GT Berlinetta he will take to third overall, while the ill-fated Alfonso de Portago loads his camera in front of his 335 S as Peter Collins looks on. The 335 S (# 534) awaits Klemantaski and Collins.

❖ Crowds along the Mille Miglia route were just as enthusiastic. *"Tremendous,"* Klemantaski said, *"All the way shouting, 'Ferrari, Ferrari,' and, of course, doing the most ludicrous things, like crossing the road."*

extensive, "By 1957 I think I had every corner noted. It was on long pages, which I rewrote, but then, of course, one put it on a roll of paper."

These days a rally driver can talk with his navigator in a whisper, thanks to noise-canceling sound systems. Fifty years ago, the only chance the pair had to communicate was to yell a few words to each other above the sound of the exhaust rattling off the walls of buildings in cities, "...but it was impossible to converse."

So how did Klemantaski communicate with Collins?

"We used hand signals and graded the corners." Klemantaski held his hand in front of Collins' face and showed one to five fingers to assign a degree of difficulty to what they faced, one for a slow corner, five meaning to go flat out.

Klemantaski knew that it was most useful for Collins if he could convey to the driver, "If you're going over a rise whether there's a corner or whether you can go flat-out.

"It was obvious that you don't signal your driver when you come to dangerous bits because there were always crowds around... hopefully."

All this says a great deal about the trust Klemantaski and Collins placed in each other.

A modern race crew would be dressed in fire-resistant suits, gloves, and shoes, scientifically designed helmets strapped to their heads, a rugged computer-configured rollcage around them. By comparison, Collins, Klemantaski, and the other competitors in the mid-1950s were downright naked. Just enough civilian clothes to be

Enzo Ferrari and test driver Martino Severi (right) discuss changes made to the shape of the gear shift knob at Peter Collins' request.

comfortable in the weather, thin leather gloves and helmets that wouldn't pass muster for today's bicycle riders.

Did it ever frighten Klemantaski?

"Never. For one thing, I knew what the next corner was going to be like from my notes and I sat there thinking, 'Go on, go on, you can get around that faster.' I mean, I wouldn't dream of doing it with anyone I didn't trust distinctly."

Then he added with a smile, "Well, I'm half of Russian descent—my mother was Russian—and they're sort of fatalistic."

Klemantaski slipped into classic British understatement by adding, "For me it was a sheer thrill, not because we went fast because ordinary cars go just as fast now, but it's the cornering when you're with a good driver and you don't have the slightest qualm. Even at Peter Collins' speeds I never, never once had any serious misgivings about the next corner. I just sat back and enjoyed the cornering and acceleration as a continuous thrill."

What was the best part?

"I think the Adriatic straights, because there we were going along mile after mile and I knew there wasn't any corner. Villages didn't count, you still went flat out. And minute after minute we were sitting there, Peter was just like that (imitates Collins calmly holding the steering wheel) and we were doing 180 mph. And I don't suppose they do much more now days in sports racing cars (and certainly not on tires that narrow or on roads that are rough and highly crowned).

"One did look at the countryside when one was on long straights. There's one on the way back from Rome, I forget the name of it, and there are several lakes and there's one little lake with an island in the middle." That was in 1957, when Collins stood a good chance of winning the Formula 1 world championship. "Somehow or other he found time on this easy bit of road to say to me, 'If I win the championship, I'm going to buy that island and go and live there.'"

Sadly, Collins never won his championship and was killed in a Ferrari Grand Prix car in the 1958 German Grand Prix.

Ferraris weren't trucked to Brescia for the Mille Miglia but driven, and Klemantaski recalled that when they were at Maranello, Enzo Ferrari, "...was very fond of Peter. When he was at the works he would come out or he'd call Peter into his office.

"The best part was when you'd take the car up to the mountains behind Ferrari before going to Brescia and then all the little urchins and everybody would be lining the road just to see a Ferrari come out of the factory gates."

Crowds along the Mille Miglia route were just as enthusiastic.

"Tremendous," Klemantaski said, "All the way shouting, 'Ferrari, Ferrari,' and, of course, doing the most ludicrous things, like crossing the road. On one long straight road, one was flat out and the people were standing not

only on the verge but actually in the road and you had just enough room to go through."

Tough enough in a red car, but when he was in the green Aston Martin chasing a Ferrari, "The red car would go through and the crowd would all step into the road and look after it. There you were coming up from behind, and it was terrifying. Blowing the horn, flashing the lights, and they always managed to just step back. But, of course, what could you do? If you're in a race you can't take your foot off just for those people. . .

"When we were in a green car (the Aston), if you came to a level (railroad) crossing the arm would come down. When we were in the Ferrari," Klemantaski chuckled, "they more or less stopped the train." **F**

Peter Sachs driving and Louis Klemantaski navigating in the 335 S, which Ferrari World Champion Phil Hill considers the greatest of Maranello's front-engine race cars.

• Dan Gurney on the 375 Plus Spider
Race driver and team owner, motorcycle manufacturer
Santa Ana, California

DAN GURNEY STARTED HIS ROAD RACING IN A TRIUMPH TR-2 IN 1955, PROGRESSED TO A PORSCHE Speedster, and even raced a Denzel. None of these were exactly tire-burners. Just two years later, he was at the other end of the horsepower scale in a Ferrari.

Built in 1954, Ferrari's 375 Plus Spider was powered by a 4.9-liter Lampredi V-12 with a claimed 330 horsepower.

Car number 0478 AM was originally entered in Southern California races by Tony Parravano, a building contractor with a stable of great race cars. A mysterious man under the microscope of Federal investigators, Parravano just disappeared one day.

The 4.9 Ferrari was bought by Frank Arciero, who was starting a race team that has become well-known in the U.S. One of Arciero's shrewd early moves was to give young Dan Gurney a drive.

Gurney remembers: "The 4.9 was notoriously kind of viscous, so when the time came for Bob Drake to drive that or an Aston Martin, he chose to drive the Aston. Which meant Frank Arciero was looking for a driver."

He called Gurney, who agreed, and Arciero asked, "Would you come to Willow Springs, where we're going to test?"

"At Willow [a road course in the Antelope Valley east of Los Angeles], there was a parking area next to the track that was paved. I got in the 4.9 and started spinning donuts, trying to get a feel for how the car did or didn't hook up getting the power on the ground.

"That particular car was not good at all in that area, though it was doggone fast and would run over 180 mph, which in those days was plenty quick.

"One of the reasons I think Bob decided to drive the Aston Martin was because you could have some opposite lock, gas it, and still have the car work with you. Well, the 4.9 wouldn't. It would spin the tires and you'd be in trouble. So what do you do?

"In those days you couldn't say, 'Hey, send a race engineer over here to tell me what to do because this thing is kind of lethal.' Your only option was to adapt your driving to the car.

"In corners, we used a technique that used to be called 'diamonding' the turn. Instead of trying to maintain high speed all the way around the corner, you came in and made a little bit of a late apex that was pretty tight. You could have almost a straight exit and that's how you had to drive the 4.9. If you could get the power down without spinning the tires—which you couldn't do unless you were halfway straight—it was a fast car.

"On that occasion I set a lap record at Willow that lasted for three years or so. Now it's amazingly slow—something like 1 minute, 42.9 seconds—and a modern street car can go around faster than that.

"I drove the car for Frank, did well, finished second in a couple of races, and later beat Carroll Shelby in his 4.9 at Palm Springs."

It turns out that Luigi Chinetti was keeping track of things and invited Gurney to race at Le Mans in 1958. A few months later the 27-year-old driver was really in the pressure cooker.

"In November 1958 I was invited to the Modena Autodromo. I met Enzo Ferrari there on a gray, cold day and the Ferrari transporter arrived with three race cars: a 2.0-liter sports car, a 3.0-liter Testa Rossa Le Mans car, and a 2.5-liter Grand Prix car. It dawned on me that I was the only driver in the place and here were Enzo and his engineers with their black fedoras and overcoats.

"I had asked for help from some guys like Hans Tanner and Peter Coltrin—who had been staying at the Albergo Real hotel—for some advice on what I should do in the try-out. They said, 'Go as fast as you can and don't make any mistakes.'"

So much for seeking sage advice.

"I drove the 2.0-liter sports car as fast as I dared, then graduated to the 3.0-liter Le Mans car, and finally into the Formula I Ferrari with Enzo and his race people eye-balling everything.

"At the end of that I didn't know if I had succeeded or failed and they didn't indicate anything except to say: 'Be ready the day after tomorrow. We're going to Monza to test the Le Mans car.'

"At Monza, the Ferrari test driver was the only other driver and he knew the track like the back of his hand. It was a foggy, moist day and it was raining. I had one of those Herbert Johnson helmets and did what I could to see. That car would run 150 mph by the time you got to the Curva Grande.

✤ *"The 4.9 was notoriously kind of viscous, so when the time came for Bob Drake to drive that or an Aston Martin, he chose to drive the Aston."* — Dan Gurney

"It took me quite some time to equal the test driver's time, but I did. I also spun the car in the Parabolica on my cool off lap, but didn't go off the track, so I never said anything to them.

"I was by myself and the stress level was pretty high. I found out some time later that, in fact, I passed the test and I was offered a job for 1959. I started at Sebring and got my first Formula I drive in mid-season. First race I dropped out with a hole in my radiator, the second race I finished second, the third I finished thurd and in the fourth I was fourth."

We all know where Gurney went from there… ⟨F⟩

Dan Gurney drove a Ferrari 4.9-liter 375 Plus for Frank Arciero at Riverside (left) and at Palm Springs (below) where he won on his 27th birthday. Gurney earned a place on the Ferrari Formula I team (right), shown here adjusting his helmet while the famous Luigi Bazzi works on his car.

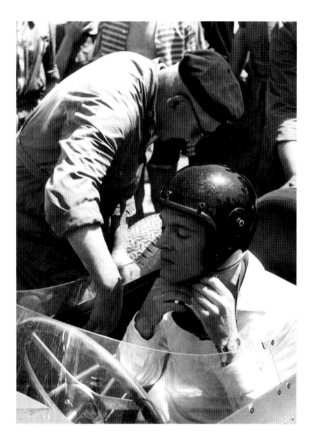

Grand Prix

GRAND PRIX RACING
Fours, eights, and sixes.

FERRARI'S FIRST ATTEMPTS TO BEAT HIS RIVAL ALFA ROMEO'S ALFETTA WERE WITH the Colombo supercharged V-12-powered 125, and they weren't successful. This was one of the major arguments for Lampredi's non-supercharged big-block V-12, and while Alfa dominated the 1950 Grand Prix season, the unblown Ferraris finally beat them the next season.

Previous pages: Mike Hawthorn in a Ferrari 246 F1 in the 1958 Belgian Grand Prix. Below, Lancia had the great Vittorio Jano design its D50 Grand Prix. The V-8-powered car proved very quick, but the death of its main driver, the great Alberto Ascari (who died while testing a Ferrari sports car), and the financial drain of racing caused Lancia to back out of Formula 1 and the cars went to Ferrari. Juan Manuel Fangio drove such a car to win the 1956 World Championship for Maranello. Seen with the D50 is another famous Italian race car, the 1907 Fiat that Felice Nazarro drove to win that year's French Grand Prix.

Motoring journalist Paul Frère figures that was the turning point for Ferrari: "When (Froilán) Gonzáles beat (Juan Manuel) Fangio (in an Alfa) at Silverstone in 1951, that was global news… followed by… the complete supremacy of Ferrari the two following years."

Alfa quit Grand Prix racing after 1951 and with a lack of proper Formula 1 cars for 1952, the GP events reverted to Formula 2 rules. Ferrari was ready with Lampredi's 4-cylinder 2.0-liter machines and Alberto Ascari went on to win the World Driver's Championship in 1952 and 1953.

There were new rules for 1954, getting back to proper Formula 1, now with 2.5-liter engines. Ferrari had a car called the 553 F1, here the numbers meaning a 6-cylinder engine with a displacement of 2.5 liters, a numbering system used initially with Ferrari sixes. Called the Squalo, it was an ugly car with ugly results. Ferrari won only three races in 1954 and 1955 against Mercedes-Benz and Maserati, the latter racing its new 250F, which was designed by none other than Gioacchino Colombo.

1950 166 F2

1951 375 Indy

1950 340 F1

1954 553 F1 Squalo

At the end of the 1955 season, Ferrari took over the Lancia team's D50 race cars, getting engineer Vittorio Jano in the deal. Fangio won the 1956 driver's championship for Maranello.

But Fangio went back to Maserati in 1957 to win another driver's crown in the 250F and Ferrari didn't get a single win in the now-outdated D50-based machines.

Below, vintage race specialist Willie Green driving a 1960 Ferrari 246 Formula 1 car.

For 1958 Ferrari began anew. Carlo Chiti (with input from Jano) created the 246 GP car with a V-6 named Dino after Ferrari's recently deceased son. They hit the bull's eye, Mike Hawthorn winning the driver's championship… only to retire from racing and then die in a road accident the following January.

This was a deadly era in racing, and Ferrari team drivers Peter Collins and Luigi Musso had both died in racing accidents in 1958. For the next year the team used several drivers: Phil Hill, Dan Gurney, Tony Brooks, Jean Behra, Cliff Allison, Olivier Gendebien, and Wolfgang von Trips. Brooks nearly won the driver's championship with the front-engine Ferrari 246 Dino, but lost to Jack Brabham in a rear-engine Cooper. The writing was on the wall for the front-engine F1 race cars. **F**

A green Ferrari? British driver Peter Whitehead bought this 1949 Ferrari 125 Grand Prix car and painted it in his country's national racing colors. The Ferrari had a supercharged 1.5-liter Colombo V-12 rated by the factory at 280 horsepower, but came with an additional 2.0-liter non-supercharged engine so it could be raced in Formula 2. A subsequent owner pulled the V-12 in favor of a Chevrolet V-8. This was the first car bought by Englishman Tom Wheatcroft when he established his now-famous Donington Collection of vintage race cars, and he managed to find the original V-12 and make the famous green Ferrari complete once again.

The lineup of Ferraris at the 1953 German Grand Prix (left), held at the Nürburgring. These were the 2.0-liter 4-cylinder Formula 2 cars that competed for the championship, as there was no Formula 1 in 1952 and 1953. Helmeted Giuseppe "Nino" Farina, the first World Champion (1950), talks with Ferrari team manager Mino Amorotti. Above: Amorotti and mechanic Luigi Parenti check the fuel level in the Ferrari of Alberto Ascari, who is signing an autograph. This race would be Farina's first win for Ferrari, though Ascari would win the driver's championship in 1953, just as he did in 1952.

The 1960s

The 1960s

PRODUCTION CARS
A decade of great design

FERRARI BEGAN THE 1960S WITH THE CONSERVATIVE 250 GT DESIGN AND continued in that vein when it launched the 250 GT 2+2 with a small rear seat.

But Pininfarina was proving it was capable of more pizzazz with its Superfast II, III, and IV show cars and a limited series of 400 SA (and, later, 500 Superfast) "aerodinamico" coupes.

The design firm proved its worth once again at the 1962 Paris Auto Show when Ferrari presented the 250 GT Berlinetta Lusso with an exquisite shape derived from Maranello race cars. The 2+2 line shed some of its conservativeness in late 1963 with the 330 GT 2+2. The 330 in the name signaled Ferrari's move away from the now-classic 250 GT 3.0-liter V-12 to almost four liters.

Previous pages: The Ferrari 250 TR61 that Phil Hill and Olivier Gendebien drove to win the 1961 24 Hours of Le Mans. Below: The 250 GT Lusso.

Ferrari's 250 GT 2+2 was Maranello's first 4-seater produced in large numbers.

At the Paris show in 1964, Ferrari unveiled two new cars: the 275 GTB, which replaced the Lusso, and a Spider called the 275 GTS. Both had 3.3-liter V-12s, with independent rear suspension replacing the traditional Ferrari live rear axles.

In what nowadays would be called a product offensive, Ferrari unveiled two more new models at the Geneva show the following spring. One, the 330 GTC, was a high perform-ance two-seater with a bit more luxury. The styling is a bit understated, but the total package of design along with its independent suspension and 4.0-liter V-12 make this one of the great Ferraris of the 1960s. Ditto with the GTS, essentially a convertible version of the GTC that appeared late in 1966. They would be even faster in 1969 when they received 4.4-liter engines to become the 365 GTS/GTC.

At the same 1966 show where the GTC was presented, Ferrari also offered the 365 California, a long, open machine that some would consider a bit over styled.

Quickest of the 250 GT SWBs were the SEFAC versions built in 1961 to race at Le Mans (above). They featured light-weight aluminum bodies and added horsepower for their V-12s. Below is one of the most exciting Pininfarina designs for road-going Ferraris, the "aerodinamico" coupe on the 400 Superamerica chassis. This particular 400 SA is one of few Ferraris first registered to Enzo Ferrari.

To appeal to those who wanted to carry more than two, Ferrari had the large, impressive-looking 365 2+2 in 1967. At the other end of the size scale came the Dino 206 with its 2.0-liter V-6 mounted behind the passenger compartment.

Oddly enough, while the 275 GTB in its two- and four-camshaft versions is highly prized today, it wasn't a hot seller in the 1960s. Luigi Chinetti tried to bump sales with a convertible version called the NART Spider, and the 10 that were made are now prized.

Ferrari and Pininfarina put their trust in 26-year-old designer Leonardo Fioravanti to come up with a solution, and he did so in just in a week: the 365 GTB/4. Otherwise known as the Daytona, the 365 GTB/4 was almost an instant classic.

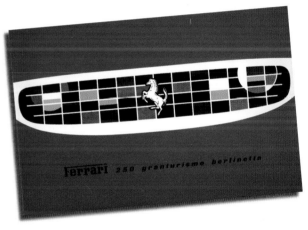

Any number of automotive designers will tell you the Pininfarina-designed Ferrari 250 GT SWB (top) is one of the best car shapes of the post-World War II era. First shown at the Paris Auto Show in 1959, they went on sale in 1960 with 280-horse-power V-12 engines. Ferrari's 250 GT California Spiders, like the one at the left, were done with steel or aluminum bodies. Below left is a 275 GTB that is unique because Battista Pininfarina owned it.

• Giorgetto Giugiaro
Designer
Torino, Italy

Giorgetto Giugiaro shaped the body of the 250 GT above for his then-boss, Nuccio Bertone, in 1962.

GIORGETTO GIUGIARO MAY BE THE MOST PROLIFIC AND SUCCESSFUL AUTOMOTIVE DESIGNER OF THE past half century. The Italian has penned entire lines of automobiles for companies such as Fiat, Maserati, SEAT, and Volkswagen. He did the original Lexus GS, and who knows how many other cars he has clothed that he isn't allowed to mention?

Giugiaro even shaped the exterior design of Nikon's F3, F4, F5, and F6 professional cameras.

The designer's career has taken him to Fiat, Bertone, Ghia, and then to his own firm, Italdesign, founded in 1969. Some might notice that Pininfarina, which has shaped the bodies of most Ferraris for more than 60 years, is missing from the list.

But Giugiaro has penned Ferraris. Explains the famed designer: "My first contact with the world of Ferrari dates back to the early years of my career as a car designer.

"I moved to Carrozzeria Bertone and in November 1959 at the Turin Show, we showcased both the Alfa Romeo 2000/2600 Sprint and a one-off version on a tubular chassis No. 1739 of the Ferrari 250 GT, ordered by a private Italian customer.

"This unique one-off special, a 2+2 coupé, was characterized by clean, crisp, elegantly styled, sporting and penetrating lines, highlighted by a rather long bonnet and a light roof resting on slim pillars.

"Innovative construction details included integration of the entire front part—bonnet and mudguards—in a single piece, hinged at the front.

"I remember that Nuccio Bertone wanted to use pearlescent paints made of fish scales."

Giugiaro came closest to designing a production Ferrari with the unusual and highly original Ferrarina, which was to become the ASA 1000 Coupé prototype, which the Modena-based firm ordered from Nuccio Bertone. It was a compact GT fitted with a 1031cc, 98-horsepower, 4-cylinder Ferrari engine. It made its debut in 1961,

❖ *"I tried to reflect the styling cues of the Formula 1*
Ferraris at the front. We introduced a nose with a double wedge-shaped radiator
grille." — *Giorgetto Giugiaro*

then was passed to the Milan-based ASA company of the De Nora family, which also developed roadster and racing versions.

"I can say that this model is linked very closely to Ferrari's image, especially for its low, 'squashed' radiator grille, its wraparound headlights, the line of the entire front and for its fastback tail," Giugiaro says.

The Ferrarina was a pretty little coupe, but fewer than 100 were built.

Giugiaro says "I dedicated all my attention to designing another Ferrari prototype—not ordered by Modena—desired by Nuccio Bertone for his personal use: the Ferrari 250 GT Bertone, which aroused great interest at the 1962 Turin Show.

"I tried to reflect the styling cues of Formula 1 Ferraris at the front. We introduced a nose with a double wedge-shaped radiator grille, still low but much lighter compared with the ASA 1000, which terminated enveloping the headlights on the mudguard.

"In my opinion, viewed three-quarter-wise, the seamless line between the crest of the rear mudguard, the downward swoop of the sloping rear window, and the area of the boot was a very successful styling statement. The result also reflected the typical styling cues of English sports cars, very popular at that time.

"Due to the privileged relationship that existed between Ferrari and Pininfarina, which was to spawn many exceptional styling and commercial successes for many years, I and Italdesign were not involved in any Ferrari order. This probably explains why, in order to commemorate my 50 years in the world of car design, I decided to design a personal Ferrari, an exclusive 'jewel' to be preserved.

"Very precise agreements were reached with Ferrari, which declared that it would be pleased to make available the chassis and mechanicals of the 612 Scaglietti four-seater 12-cylinder coupé provided that the prototype did not contrast with Ferrari's own sales strategies and was not presented as a possible production car.

"Therefore, having to comply with

marketing restraints and wishing to avoid a formula that could be considered provocative or 'disturbing,' when designing the Ferrari GG 50, I decided to transfer the parameters and values I have always tried to adopt on all my models, regardless of the segment to which they belong, to a mythical marque that epitomizes the concept of sportiness. I avoid excess, concentrate on elegant lines and proportions, offer the driver and passengers the best possible comfort, and refocus attention on the cab and the human element, especially when this has reached maturity and a certain existential equilibrium.

"After conceiving of the general design of the proportions, I hope they comply with the tastes and expectations of fans of the 'Prancing Horse.'

"When guests join me in 'my' Ferrari, I always draw their attention to the seats and the space inside the cab, which is generous for a four-seater. I have reduced the overall length of the car by 90mm, but there is still a large amount of space available for stowing luggage. The backs of the rear seats can be folded down, thanks to the redesigned fuel tank, to create a 55-inch deep flat load platform with a total capacity of 17.6 cubic feet.

"How does it feel to design a Ferrari? It's the same emotion that's experienced when driving a Ferrari." ▣

Enzo Ferrari gave a 250 GT chassis to Nuccio Bertone and the head of the famous design firm had his young chief designer, Giorgetto Giugiaro, create the body. The front reflects the twin-nostril nose of Ferrari race cars of the era.

Giugiaro went on to establish his own company, Italdesign, which has created designs for automakers around the world. To celebrate his 50 years in the business, Giugiaro did the same as his former employer, creating a Ferrari of his own, the GG 50, below, which is based on the platform of a 612 Scaglietti.

By the end of the 1960s, the era of one-off show cars for customers was about over. But Pininfarina had a new act ready, a series of dramatic show cars meant as design studies, the first of what we call concept cars today.

There were studies that pointed at the upcoming Dino, like the 1967 Dino Competizione, plus the 1967 365 P with a center-driver and three-across seating that predated the McLaren F1 by several decades. There was the futuristic 1968 250 P5 and then the P6, the styling prototype for the mid-engine Berlinetta Boxer production car in the 1970s.

All promises of things to come in the next decade. ◪

Pininfarina created many Ferrari show cars during the 1960s. At the right is the Dino Competizione from the 1967 Frankfurt Motor Show, with gullwing doors and front and rear spoilers. Below is the three-across seating in the 1966 Paris Show's 365 P. Based on a mid-engine sports racing chassis from 1965, this is one of three similar cars built by Pininfarina, one going to Fiat chief Giovanni Agnelli. Below, right, is the Geneva Show car from 1968, the Ferrari 250 P5.

SPORTS RACING CARS
Mid-engine revolution

FERRARI BEGAN THE 1960S IN TRADITIONAL FASHION WITH ITS 3.0-LITER V-12
Testa Rossas, which were still strong enough to win the constructors' championship. They
also won the 24 Hours of Le Mans with Olivier Gendebien and Paul Frère. "We led for 22 of
the 24 hours," recalls Frère. "That we won in a Ferrari was important because everyone knows
and admires Ferrari and if I had won it in a Jaguar, for instance, nobody would remember."

But it was obvious there had to be changes, not only as the sports car world moved to
mid-engine cars, but also in improving the Ferraris' aerodynamics.

This made 1961 an evolutionary year, Ferrari racing both the front-engine 250 V-12 Testa
Rossa and the mid-engine 246 V-6 Dino machines. Both had new bodywork shaped for

continued on page 106

When asked which Ferrari engine is the best, famed race driver and motoring journalist Paul Frère says, "For me it will always be the 3.0-liter V-12 of the end of the 1950s and early 1960s. It was smooth, flexible and powerful, and engines developing 100 horsepower per liter in those times were quite rare."

• Paul Frère on Ferrari's Conservative Nature

Racing driver and journalist
Monaco

ENZO FERRARI WAS KNOWN FOR HIS CONSERVATIVE APPROACH TO RACE CAR DESIGN, PUTTING HIS emphasis on great engines. Or so it seemed in 1960.

Paul Frère is a legend. An engineer and motoring journalist, he was also a great race driver in the 1950s and 1960s. Among other racing accomplishments, Frère finished second with a Ferrari in the 1956 Belgian Grand Prix on the very fast and dangerous Spa circuit, and won the 24 Hours of Le Mans in a Testa Rossa with fellow Belgian, Olivier Gendebien, in 1960.

He has a keen recall of it all, even in his 90th year. Frère says that because Ferrari was not an engineer, he was very conservative. "I remember that after I won Le Mans I had an interview with him and I said, 'Most of your competitors now use fuel injection for their engines. Why do you continue to use carburetors?'

"Ferrari answered, 'Look, if we all had fuel injection from the beginning and if today someone came with something as simple and efficient as the carburetor, everyone would change to the carburetor.'

"Ferrari and most Italian racing car manufacturers concentrated on the engine," Frère explains. "They had no interest and no knowledge at all of how a chassis works." He then adds, "One thing that prevented the Italians of those times from coming up with new technology was the fact they only spoke Italian."

Frère then mentions the theories of Maurice Olley, an Englishman who worked at General Motors and was one of the first Corvette engineers: "It's very simple: a theory about cars oversteering, cars understeering, or being neutral.

"How do you make a car understeer, which is necessary for high-speed stability? You make the roll stiffness of the front axle stronger than the rear axle. And vice versa. That's a very simple theory. Olley's papers were published in, I believe, 1934, and in 1936 all General Motors cars came with an anti-roll bar in the front axle.

"Apparently they had never heard of it 20 years later in Italy."

The most classic examples of Ferrari's conservative approach are from the late 1950s, when he was criticized for his slow conversion from drum to disc brakes and the movement to mid-engine race cars. But he was changing.

Frère describes his winning Ferrari 250 Testa Rossa from Le Mans in 1960 as being extremely slow on the straight because that year the rules required that the windshield must be 25 centimeters high.

"Ferrari had just rigged up a higher windscreen, where people like Jaguar and Maserati had studied the case and aerodynamically developed their cars."

Paul Frère co-drove to victory at Le Mans for Ferrari in 1960 and is renowned for his decades as an insightful motoring journalist.

Frère asked Ferrari, "Why don't you take more care of your cars' aerodynamics? I timed my car myself during the race and it did, full blast, 259 km/h (161 mph) while Jaguars were doing 275–280 (170–174 mph)?"

Ferrari gave him the classic answer: "You know, Frère, aerodynamics are for people who can't make good engines."

But, it turns out, Ferrari was considering changes. Frère recounts that, "Many years later, I met [Giotto] Bizzarrini at the London airport and we both had two hours to wait. I told him that story."

The highly regarded engineer in charge of developing Ferrari's race cars at the time of Frère's Le Mans win, Bizzarrini told Frère, "After you'd been in Maranello, Ferrari sent me out to time the car on the autostrada and I timed anything between 258 and 260 km/h (160 and 162 mph)."

A few days later Ferrari called Bizzarrini back and said, "I would like you to check the engine testing facilities and try to check if everything is in order and people aren't trying to fool me with the power of our engines." After everyone had left the factory Bizzarrini went to the testing rooms and found things were in order and reported that to Ferrari.

Ferrari said, "Then you should take care of the cars' aerodynamics."

All you need to do is look at the difference in the shape of Ferrari sports cars from 1960 to 1961 to see the changes. Some of that new

✤ *"Ferrari and most Italian racing car manufacturers concentrated on the engine."* — *Paul Frère*

direction flows from the gradual change to mid-engine race cars, but even in the form of the front-engine 1961 Le Mans-winning Testa Rossa you can see Enzo Ferrari was not afraid of change.

Ferraris certainly weren't perfect, but there now seemed to be permission to delve into change, as witnessed at a test session at Monza in 1961 when American driver (and technical wizard) Richie Ginther tried an experiment that led to the modern adoption of spoilers. ▣

Paul Frère, co-driving with fellow Belgian Olivier Gendebien, leaves the pits for the last time on his way to victory in the Ferrari 250 Testa Rossa 59/60 during the 24 Hours of Le Mans on June 26, 1960.

Ferrari's last front-engine sports racing car was this hot rod built for the 1962 24 Hours of Le Mans in which Phil Hill and Olivier Gendebien drove the car to an overall win. Called a 330 TRI/LM, it is basically an older Testa Rossa that was rebuilt with its chassis lengthened. Also, it had a 4.0-liter V-12 and a new body by Fantuzzi.

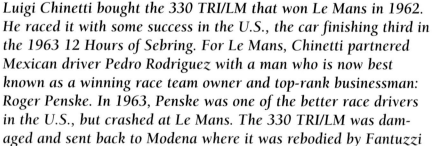

Luigi Chinetti bought the 330 TRI/LM that won Le Mans in 1962. He raced it with some success in the U.S., the car finishing third in the 1963 12 Hours of Sebring. For Le Mans, Chinetti partnered Mexican driver Pedro Rodriguez with a man who is now best known as a winning race team owner and top-rank businessman: Roger Penske. In 1963, Penske was one of the better race drivers in the U.S., but crashed at Le Mans. The 330 TRI/LM was damaged and sent back to Modena where it was rebodied by Fantuzzi

as a coupe (above, left). When finished it was bought by Hisashi Okada of Long Island, New York, who used it for daily commuting into Manhattan for years. In 1974, Okada traded the car to Ferrari collector Pierre Bardinon in France for a Ferrari 250 LM. Bardinon shipped the coupe back to Modena, where the coupe body was removed and put on another older Ferrari chassis. Fantuzzi then rebuilt the 330 TRI/LM to look as it did when it won Le Mans.

While the car at the left is the last front-engine Ferrari sports racing car, the one on this page is Maranello's first mid-engine sports racer, a 246 SP with a 2.4-liter V-6. Bearing serial number 0790, it was used at the 1961 press conference when Enzo Ferrari announced the new mid-engine cars. While testing at Monza in March that year, Richie Ginther tried some experiments with 0790 that led to the modern age of race car spoilers. This car was used to win the 1961 Targa Florio and the 1962 1000-kilometer Nürburgring race, along the way swapping its original dual-snout nose for the one seen here. Converted to a 2.0-liter 196 SP, it had a strong hillclimb career in Europe. Now in the U.S., 0790 is actively raced by its owner, Chuck Wegner, in Ferrari's Shell Historic Challenge Series. And while the 196 SP has been mechanically maintained, it has thankfully never been restored.

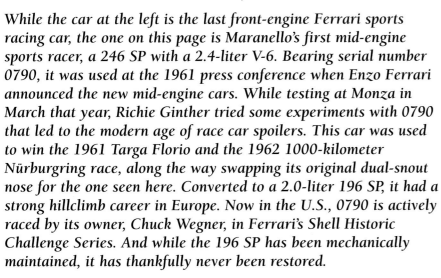

• Sergio Scaglietti and the 250 GTO

Retired
Modena, Italy

Sergio Scaglietti is the designer of Ferrari's 250 GTO, one of the most prized automobiles in the world.

WALKING INTO A MODERN AUTOMOTIVE DESIGN STUDIO CAN BE A BIT LIKE ENTERING THE BRIDGE OF the *Starship Enterprise* from *Star Trek*. Computers everywhere. Alcoves with people wearing headsets examining virtual-reality automobiles.

You likely wouldn't be working here unless you have a degree from one of the major design or technical schools. There's little chance you'd be a guy whose formal education stopped at age 13 when you started working in a mechanical workshop doing odd jobs and learning how to use a hammer and your native skills and talent to shape metal.

Ironically, if you worked in that highly computerized design center shaping modern cars, there's little chance you'd have the opportunity to create one of the world's most sensuous and beautiful automobiles.

But this kid who started in the workshop doing odd jobs went on to create the body for Ferrari's 250 GTO.

At 87 years old, Sergio Scaglietti has cut back to smoking just 15 Camels each day. The habit didn't seem to have slowed him when we met on a cold December day in Modena.

Scaglietti's name is on the building where hundreds of Ferrari bodies have been made. He sold the firm to the automaker, and Ferrari's latest 2+2 model is called the 612 Scaglietti in his honor.

It hasn't gone to his head, and he speaks in a quiet, almost humble manner about how they built bodies for Ferrari.

He started his firm in 1951, and by the middle of the decade was doing much of Ferrari's bodywork. Scaglietti gets the credit for the headrests on Ferrari race cars and also for the famous pontoon fenders on the 1958 customer Testa Rossas, a shape meant to help cool the drum brakes.

He simply explains, "My work was to build and to bang the sheet metal. At that time it was very difficult to work with aluminum." There are old stories about how Ferrari bodies were formed over wood, but Scaglietti explains, "We formed the aluminum over bags of sand. Wood is too hard, you destroy the aluminum, but the sand will move." And they did all their work, "by the eye."

Generally, wooden models of new Ferraris would arrive from Pininfarina. Based on these, Scaglietti would create a framework of 6 mm wire that was used as the form to check the body panels as they were made.

But the GTO was all Scaglietti.

Until the 1962 racing season, championship points in the international sports car series were awarded for open sports racing cars. As of 1962, those "pure" racers could still run for the overall win, but series points would go to closed, more-streetable Grand Touring cars.

Race drivers weren't all that excited about the championship being for GTs, but the move did create some wonderful automobiles, like Aston Martin's DB4GT Zagato, lightweight Jaguar E-Types, Porsche 904s, and Ferrari's 250 GTO.

Only 36 GTOs were built and all but a few have Scaglietti's famous Series 1 body shape. They are among the most treasured automobiles in the world and you can't buy one for less than $10 million, probably more.

Which makes it all the more interesting when you ask Sergio Scaglietti how he decided on the car's design and he says, "It was quite easy."

Scaglietti got a chassis from Ferrari that he describes as, "a mess," and he had to make the car's internal structure from very light tubing.

Where did he get inspiration?

"By looking at cars," he says, "Just looking… with the eye… if you use your head, knowing the car has to go fast, you make it smaller and lighter." He created the shape with no plans, no drawings and no clay models, making the framework that would be the shape with his eye and forming the aluminum around it. Scaglietti adds that the men who worked with him were fantastic.

Today race cars like the 250 GTO would be sent straight to a wind tunnel for aerodynamic testing, but Scaglietti didn't have any such facility. They essentially had a big fan in front of the car and blew the air over the racing car, checking fabric tufts attached to the sheet metal to see how they reacted to the flow.

Tell this to a young computer-driven designer and he'll just shake his head in amazement… and wish he had the chance to do the same.

Incidentally, to Sergio Scaglietti, the most beautiful cars he built were the 275 GTBs.

He is amazed by the automation in the factory that now carries his name. His firm was able to make only one body each day, but the current factory can produce dozens, with all the workers dressed in white.

As for using a modern software program to design a car on a flat screen, Scaglietti says, "I don't even know what a computer is." ▣

❖ *"By looking at cars, just looking… with the eye… if you use your head, knowing the car has to go fast, you make it smaller and lighter."* — Sergio Scaglietti

Scaglietti's name is still over the factory (left) where Ferrari makes advanced aluminum automobiles. Below is the first of Scaglietti's 250 GTOs, chassis 3223. Phil Hill (left), who co-drove 3223 to win its first time out, talks with Carlo Chiti, who managed the Ferrari team at the time. On the following pages is a display of the 20 250 GTOs present at the 2004 Rolex Monterey Historic Automobile Races.

So many 250 GTOs have great stories, including serial number 3589. It was first raced by Mike Parkes for Tommy Sopwith, then by Innes Ireland (seen above) for Tom O'Conner's Texas-based Rosebud Racing team. In 1964, O'Conner gave the GTO to the Victoria High School, which sold it 8 years later. The next owner apparently put it on a trailer and kept it in a field. In the late 1980s the GTO was rescued and restored.

Though it's a short-wheelbase 250 GT under the skin, this is considered to be the prototype for the 250 GTO. The body style is that of Pininfarina's Superfast II series and the V-12 is the same type used in the GTO. The car first caught every-one's eye when Stirling Moss used it to win his class in the 1962 Daytona Continental.

This very unusual Ferrari is a short-wheelbase 250 GT that was rebodied in 1962 by Piero Drogo with a shape that has caused it to be nicknamed the "Breadvan."

Ferrari's second series of GTOs had a new shape that looks a bit faster than the original, but loses that shape's sensuousness.

This may look like a Ferrari 330 LMB, but is actually a 250 GTO.

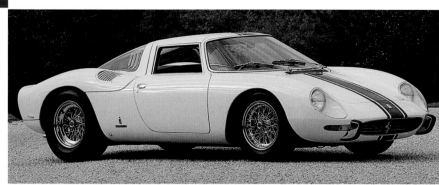

Pininfarina built this Ferrari 250 LM as a show car for the 1965 Geneva and New York Auto shows. Unlike the 250 LM race cars, it has a rear Plexiglas window that stretches out to the tail, power windows, and this delicious red interior. Below is the four-page sales brochure that was written in Italian, English, and French.

BERLINETTA   250 / LE MANS

continued from page 91

better aerodynamics and featuring a distinctive twin-nostril nose. The combination of V-12 and V-6 machines was enough to bring another constructors' championship.

This same mix continued in 1962, but with an important change. While the sports racing cars still competed for overall wins, championship points were given to the Grand Touring cars. For this Ferrari created one of its greatest race machines ever, the 250 GTO. This beautiful coupe was in many ways a 250 Testa Rossa with a closed, flowing Scaglietti-shaped body and it often vied for the race lead, allowing Ferrari to take the constructors' crown once again.

And again in 1963, thanks to the GTO, with Ferrari also winning races outright with a new sports racing car, the mid-engine V-12 250 P. There was, however, a new and threatening force: Carroll Shelby's Cobras and the looming specter of Ford in racing. Following the 250 P, from 1964 through 1967, Ferrari had a series of sports racing cars in the P series, culminating in the 330 P4, one of the most luscious race cars ever made.

Emphasis and points reverted to these open-cockpit race cars and Ferrari won the title every year but 1966, when Ford took it, just as the American company also won the 24 Hours of Le Mans in 1966, 1967, 1968, and 1969.

Ferrari's venerable warhorse of the decade proved to be the 250 LM mid-engine V-12 coupe, which won Le Mans in 1965—the last time Ferrari was an overall victor in the classic—and showed up in occasional top-10 finishes throughout the rest of the 1960s.

Ferrari also took a shot at the North American Can-Am racing series with a few good results, thanks to driver Chris Amon.

continued on page 115

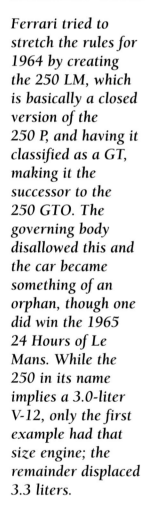

Ferrari tried to stretch the rules for 1964 by creating the 250 LM, which is basically a closed version of the 250 P, and having it classified as a GT, making it the successor to the 250 GTO. The governing body disallowed this and the car became something of an orphan, though one did win the 1965 24 Hours of Le Mans. While the 250 in its name implies a 3.0-liter V-12, only the first example had that size engine; the remainder displaced 3.3 liters.

Ferrari's 275/330 P proved to be quite successful, winning at Sebring, the Nürburgring, Le Mans, and the Tourist Trophy on the way to earning Ferrari another constructors' title in 1964. The 330 V-12 seen here was rated by the factory at 370 horsepower.

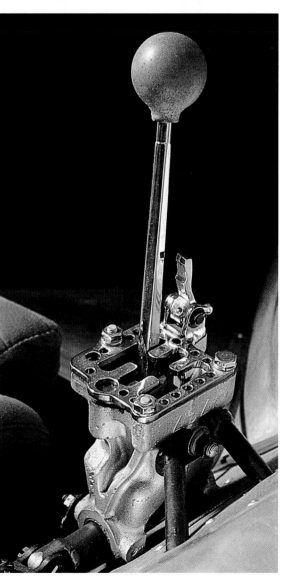

• **Carroll Shelby on the Ferrari-Ford Wars**
Race driver, 1965 GT Manufacturers' Champion
Los Angeles, Calif.

A MAN WHO HAS DONE IT ALL ISN'T AFRAID TO SPEAK HIS MIND, AND CARROLL SHELBY CERTAINLY qualifies as one of those men.

Unlike the rest of the people in this book, Shelby wasn't out to glorify Ferrari, but to beat him, both in the U.S. and in Europe, on Ferrari's home ground.

Why?

"Well, we'd beaten Corvette and I was in the business of selling cars and I figured that if you go over and beat Ferrari it would be a feather in your cap."

This is when the international sports car championship points were given to Grand Touring cars instead of sports racing prototype machines.

"I felt I could beat Ferrari with the Daytona coupe because he was hung up on 3.0 liters (the famous 3.0-liter V-12) and I had 4.7 liters with pushrods (Ford's V-8). I had him by 100 horsepower."

"In 1964, we didn't even start until June. The old Daytona coupe... shit, when we went out to Riverside the ass end came off the ground at 150 mph and by the time Phil (Remington) and the guys got to chopping it up it took about three months longer to get it to work.

"So we didn't start racing until June, raced four races and won them all and we were one point behind. The last race of the year was Monza (near Milan, Italy) and we had all six Cobras running and they were ready with new engines. We'd tested. We got to Monza and old man Ferrari got them to cancel the race." (Over a flap about homologating the mid-engine 250 LM as a production car.)

✦ *"I felt I could beat Ferrari with the Daytona coupe*
because he was hung up on 3.0 liters (the famous 3.0-liter V-12) and I had 4.7 liters with pushrods (Ford's V-8). I had him by 100 horsepower." — *Carroll Shelby*

Shelby laughs, "You know, he was the king in Italy."

Shelby then became a key player in Ford's program to win in Europe with the GT40, the main prize being the 24 Hours of Le Mans.

"Henry (Ford II) was pissed, and Don Frey (Ford's Vice President of Product Planning) says, 'Instead of developing all this stuff, let's go buy Ferrari.'

"Don Frey is still alive, and what I tell you is what he told me.

"He went over there to buy them and they set on a price of $20 million for Ferrari. Frey came back and said, 'I've got a deal,' and somebody in the controller's office said, 'Well, let's go over there and look at everything.'

"So three or four bean counters went over and, you know, they'd see a desk in a corner and say, '$25 for that? That thing isn't worth shit.' And they'd go out in the machine shop and they'd say, '$8,500 for that lathe? It's 25 years old; it's not worth anything.'

"Old man Ferrari watched that for a day or two and he said, 'Git your ass out of here.'

"Don Frey came back and said, 'Well, it's not going to work. We're going to have to build our own car. So he says to Ray Geddes and Hal Sperlich, who were working on the first Mustang then, 'Do something.'

"I said, 'Eric Broadley has a coupe he's made with a Ford engine. Let's go see if we can buy that as a prototype.' So I went to Le Mans with Ray and Hal and we made a deal right there on the spot with Broadley.

"He lasted about three months and said, 'I'm not taking this Ford shit anymore,' and left.

"We were halfway though the GT40 program when we went to Le Mans in 1965 and the engines blew up."

To rub salt into Ford's wounds, a Luigi Chinetti-entered Ferrari 250 LM—arguably somewhat past its prime at the point—won the French classic that year, driven by American Masten Gregory and Austrian Jochen Rindt.

Shelby continues, "Henry was there with his new wife and his son Edsel and said, 'Is this the best we can do?'

"Henry was embarrassed and in September of 1965 he hired Leo Beebe, who had been his commanding officer during the war, to run the deal. He had Frey, Beebe, and me in his office and he set us down and

*◆ **"The financial guy at Ford** was named Ed Lundy and at one time he said to us, 'You boys are going to break the company. You've spent over $200 million that I know of and Lord knows what I don't know about.'"* — Carroll Shelby

he had nametags 'Ford Wins in 66' with our names on them. We sat there and listened to him about 15 minutes, and later when we were walking down the hall Frey said, 'Well, he didn't say anything about our fiscal responsibility.' So we walked back in and he said, 'Mr. Ford, you didn't say anything about our fiscal responsibility.'"

Henry Ford II responded, "You boys would like a job next July 1st wouldn't you?"

"There's never been a program that didn't have a budget," Shelby responded.

At least there hadn't been until then, and Shelby tells a classic story about how determined Ford was to win in 1966: "One time at the testing in April the windshields broke. The next morning a 707 arrived at Orly field in Paris with six new windshields. That's the kind of program it was.

"The financial guy at Ford was named Ed Lundy and at one time he said to us, 'You boys are going to break the company. You've spent over $200 million that I know of and Lord knows what I don't know about.'"

Think about it—$200 million versus $20 million. **F**

Carroll Shelby (opposite page) won with Ferraris in his driving career, but as a constructor and team leader used Ford power to beat the Italian V-12 sports cars.

Carroll Shelby created the Cobra Daytona coupe (below) to harass Ferrari. It's possible to argue that Pete Brock's shape for the Cobra coupe was every bit as elegant as designs penned for Ferrari's racing GT machines.

• John Surtees MBE and the 250 P

World Driving Champion, 1964, retired
Edenbridge, Kent, Great Britain

JOHN SURTEES WAS ALREADY A GRAND PRIX MOTORCYCLE CHAMPION WHEN HE MADE THE SWITCH TO four-wheel GP machines in 1960 at the age of 26.

From the start it was obvious the transition to automobiles would be seamless for the driver, who raced a Formula I Lotus in 1960 and a Cooper in 1961.

Early on, Surtees recalls, "Ferrari made an inquiry about me and I said, 'No, no I need to get more experience before I deal with the Italians.'

"At the end of 1961 they asked me to go to Maranello and I went out there and met the old man. I saw (chief engineer) Carlo Chiti and the team and they wanted me to come, but I said no.

"They told me, 'Well, we don't ask twice. We've already asked you twice. We don't ask again.'"

Surtees declined and spent the 1962 season driving the first Lola Grand Prix car, putting it on the pole in its initial race.

After that season, "Ferrari came on again and said, 'Come see us.'"

There had been something of a palace revolt at Ferrari after Surtees' 1961 visit, and several of the key engineers had quit. "I arrived at Ferrari. Chiti had gone, and it was a new team. It was all a bit chaotic because of the people who had walked out. (Mauro) Forghieri was there, but he was like a junior engineer. Luckily (Franco) Rocchi, who had been responsible for the V-6, was still there, so I thought, why not? Here's a new beginning. Perhaps we can bring something together.

"There was a review of what we had. Michael May had come along to work on the 6-cylinder engine with direct injection. He took one of the previous year's Grand Prix cars and cobbled it around. We went down to the Modena circuit and went round and round doing as much work as we could, but only after we had a crash program to make a new prototype sports car. Formula 1 got pushed back as a secondary item.

"The new prototype sports racer was one of the previous year's V-6 models where we changed the bodywork, cut the chassis off at the engine bay, added a new frame, and stuck a Testa Rossa-type V-12 engine in it."

This was the 250 P and after still more testing laps around the track in Modena, "… it started to come around quite well. We had a rush program to get ready for Sebring because we didn't only have to build the cars for ourselves, but I needed to do the testing for the cars for (Luigi Chinetti's) NART team and for Ronnie Hoare and Maranello Concessionaires (Ferrari's importer in England).

"This was made even more annoying when I got to Sebring and I wasn't given one of the cars I tested. I, along with (Ludovico) Scarfiotti, was given the brand new car, which hadn't been tested. So I had to use practice at Sebring to sort it out. We didn't get everything done in time—witness the fact we both ended up sick because the sealing between

✚ **"The new prototype sports** *racer was one of the previous years' V-6 models where we changed the bodywork, cut the chassis off at the engine bay, added a new frame, and stuck a Testa Rossa-type V-12 engine in it.'* — *John Surtees*

the rear engine cover and the cockpit, which we'd done on the cars we tested, wasn't done and the fumes came in the cockpit."

Nonetheless, Surtees and Scarfiotti won, but came up against something several Ferrari drivers from that era could attest to: "Politics. Our team protested my win. The team did not have a lap chart but protested on the chart NART had done. Luckily, my first wife was superb in timing and lap charting and she had a full lap chart, which coincided perfectly with the organizers. And so (Ferrari team manager Eugenio) Dragoni's protest was thrown out and I think we won by a lap or something."

The well-known publication *Automobile Year* called the Dragoni protest "a lap-muddle."

"We spent a lot of time on the prototype cars… too much time to the detriment of the Formula 1 cars. But they were good, raceable, forgiving cars you could drive very hard even in places like the Nürburgring." **F**

In 1964 the 250 Ps were upgraded to 275 specifications. This 275 P is driven at Le Mans by Giancarlo Baghetti and Umberto Maglioli, but failed to finish due to an accident. Today this car sports a 330 V-12.

One of Ferrari's main weapons in the prototype war in 1965 was the 365 P/P2. This example, which features a tall, rules-required windscreen, won the 12-hour race at Reims, France.

Ferrari's 365 P/P2 was meant to be raced by the private teams that backed up the factory's effort and were equipped with carbureted 4.4-liter V-12s.

John Surtees and Ludovico Scarfiotti won the 1965 ADAC 1000km at the Nürburgring in this 330 P2.

continued from page 106

Little seen in the U.S., but causing a stir in Europe, were the ear-piercing Dino 206 2.0-liter V-6s sports racers and possibly the coolest of all small Ferraris, the 2.0-liter flat-12 212E.

Ferrari took a pass on sports car racing in 1968. Ford won the title again, and as its interest waned, Porsche was making its move from the smaller classes right to the front.

Ferrari returned in 1969 with another dramatic-looking sports racer, the 312P, and it scored well when it finished, but the company was going through a tough spell financially—Enzo Ferrari had to sell the production car side to Fiat in early 1969. F

Possibly Ferrari's most beautiful mid-engine sports racing car was the 330 P3/4. Powered by a 4.0-liter V-12, these cars were most famous for their 1-2-3 finish in the 24 Hours of Daytona in 1967, helping Ferrari secure the sports car manufacturers' championship.

In an attempt to compete in the Can-Am race series in the lucrative U.S. market, Ferrari converted 330 P3/4s into what were labeled Can-Am Spiders, but with little success.

Just as the front-engine Dino sports cars were scaled-down Testa Rossas, Ferrari's 206s were like beautiful miniaturized 330 P3/4s. With their 220-horsepower 2.0-liter engines, the mid-engine Dinos were particularly successful in hill-climbs in the hands of Ludovico Scarfiotti.

Ferrari Dino V-6 mid-engine production cars began the series of smaller models from Maranello. This is a 206 GT, and its production run began in 1967 with a 180-horsepower, 2.0-liter engine. Its successor was its 246 GT and GTS versions with 2.4-liter, 195-horse-power V-6s, and they were made until 1975 when replaced by the V-8-powered 308 GTB.

When Ferrari introduced the 330 GT2+2 in 1964 it had a 4.0-liter V-12 and four headlights, the latter taking some criticism. When the front was redone with just two lamps it became a handsome machine. This was the era when Ferrari was making the transition from wire to alloy disc wheels.

1966 330 GTC

1966 365 California

A 1969 brochure for the 365 GTC that was not imported to the United States.

1969 365 GTS/4 Daytona Spider

At the left is Ferrari's 275 GTB, which was launched in 1964 with a 260-horsepower 3.3-liter V-12. In 1966, the engine got twin camshafts per head and an increase to 280 horsepower. Below is a car that looks similar to the GTB at the left, but is quite different. Called a 275 GTB/C, it is unlike the few other models with this designation as it is closer to a 250 GTO than a GTB. The aluminum body has somewhat the same proportions of that earlier car, and like the GTOs this one has a minimal interior and a significantly more powerful V-12. This GTB/C competed in the 1965 24 Hours of Le Mans where it finished a strong third overall.

• Eddie Smith and the NART Spider

Businessman, retired
Lexington, North Carolina

To boost sales of the 275 GTB, Luigi Chinetti commissioned a convertible version. It was called the NART Spider for Chinetti's North American Racing Team and only 10 were built.

ONLY 10 FERRARI 275 GTB NART SPIDERS WERE BUILT AND IF YOU'D LIKE ONE, BE PREPARED TO WRITE A check in excess of $5 million.

Luigi Chinetti commissioned the convertible versions of the 275 GTB in 1966, the name NART standing for his North American Racing Team. Originally plans called for 25 soft-top GTBs, but only 10 were made and they have become highly prized, owned by many of the great Ferrari collectors such as Ralph Lauren and Tony Wang.

And there's still one original owner, Eddie Smith.

Eddie Smith's parents died when he was just nine, which is how he came to be in an orphanage. He'll tell you, "I got a good high school education, graduated in '37, went to Lexington (North Carolina) and got a job ushering in the theater. When I left the home they gave me $15. I got a job paying $9 and paid $5 for room and board."

Next came a job driving a cab, though Smith ended up managing the cab company. Then a position with a mail order company led to his own business in 1952 and to make a long story short, the orphan ended up owning a business

called National Wholesale Company, selling women's hosiery, lingerie, and apparel throughout the country. Smith admits, "It's been real good to us."

When his son, Eddie Jr., expressed an interest in cars, Eddie Sr. went along for the ride. They'd visit the 12 Hours of Sebring and in the process dad developed an interest in Ferraris. "I don't know just what it was, but you hear about the Ferrari mystique. You come to think it is the ultimate. It might have started in the late 1940s. I'd see on the Pathe news at the theater that Ferraris were winning."

Smith's first Ferrari was a short-wheelbase 250 GT spider followed by a 275 GTB coupe, but when he heard about the NART Spider he signed up with his friend, Luigi Chinetti, to buy one.

On the trip to Modena with Chinetti to get the car, "Luigi told me that if I decided I don't want the convertible, Steve McQueen wants it real bad. Someone has just rear ended him and totaled his car."

You can still go to Italy to get your Ferrari, but doing it with Chinetti was a different experience.

✦ *"Luigi told me* that if I decided I don't want the convertible, Steve McQueen wants it real bad. Someone has just rear ended him and totaled his car."* — Eddie Smith*

Chinetti was famous for his epic drives, like doing all but 20 minutes of the 1949 24 Hours of Le Mans, when he won for Ferrari. "He'd just drive all night long and not think a thing about it," Smith explains. "He wouldn't get tired or sleepy or anything. He'd be quiet for a while and then he would talk a bit. That was the trip where I learned that if you drive from Paris to Modena and you don't stop to eat or drink, you also don't have to stop to go to the bathroom."

Once in Modena, they would stay at the renowned Real Fini Hotel and be there a week for so, with long lunches every day.

There was no rush. Smith would ask when they were going to collect the car and return to Paris and Chinetti would ask, "You're not in a hurry, are you?"

Smith continues, "Days would go by. . . days meant nothing to him. The car was ready 2-3 days before we left." Then they would go to the factory to get the car and meet Mr. Ferrari.

Eddie Jr., who later accompanied his father to collect a Ferrari, tells, "You'd go through the archway into the courtyard and all the cars that were being delivered were waiting there. Luigi would take you on a personal tour of the factory.

"When we got to the end of the line, they put an engine on a dyno and there was a guy on the hand throttles. He fired it up, took it up to 3000 or so, backed it off, made a few adjustments or so and then he just pegged it. I was thinking that thing is going to come apart and pieces would come right through the window. I was incredulous. I looked at Luigi who seemed to know what I was thinking, and he just shrugged his shoulders and said, 'If it's going to blow, let it blow now.'"

They would then drive the Ferraris over the Alps to Paris and then have the cars shipped home.

"We weren't racing, but going quickly over the Alps. I figured if it was okay for Luigi, it was okay for us too. We just stopped for lunch, and the Italians would cheer in the small towns.

Over the years, a lot of temptations have come along to get the NART away from Smith. The first time anyone offered to buy the NART it was for $100,000, and he says, "I took a big gulp and thought to myself, 'What in the world is going on?' but I still didn't want to sell it."

Ralph Lauren came down and Smith took him for a drive in Lexington.

What was the biggest price he was ever offered? "I don't know that I've actually had a firm offer because the conversation never got that serious."

Three generations have driven the car—now with more than 40,000 miles on the odometer—with Eddie Jr.'s son, having used it on dates. "People over in High Point couldn't hardly believe it," he admits, but he let his grandson use the car for dates.

Smith explains his feelings about the Ferrari. . . echoing what a lot of owners have felt about theirs.

"I bought it for the right reasons and kept it for the right reasons. Because I really love it. I feel like it's a part of me. I just love it. I feel like I'm a part of the car. 🅵

Eddie Smith is the only original owner of a NART Spider. Smith traveled to Maranello with Luigi Chinetti to get the car. The personable Smith loves the Ferrari as much as he loves the famous barbecue in his hometown, Lexington, North Carolina.

After sitting out the 1968 season to protest rules governing international sports racing cars, Ferrari came back in 1969 with the 312 P. While the chassis and body drew from Maranello's Can-Am experience, the engine was a development of the 3.0-liter Formula 1 V-12. Raced as an open car or a coupe, the 312 Ps scored two important second-place finishes, but were no match for the Porsche 908s.

• Steven J. Earle

Founder, Rolex Monterey Historic Automobile Races
Buellton, California

STEVE EARLE—WHO FOUNDED THE MONTEREY HISTORIC AUTOMOBILE RACES AT LAGUNA SECA AND IS considered by many to be the father of vintage racing in the U.S.—has owned Ferraris for decades. And as you might expect, he has decades worth of stories to go with them. Earle has owned many of the great ones, including a 250 GTO, 512 M, and Testa Rossa.

Many years ago Earle loaned his GTO to Chuck Queener, the graphic designer of this book, and me so we could drive it into the hills north of Los Angeles and photograph it with the GTO of his old friend, Chris Cord. Thanks, Steve. We really had a great time with your car.

Once, after we photographed Earle's pontoon-fendered Testa Rossa at his home, he put a new battery in the ex-Roger Penske 512 M, which was in his garage, just to fire it up for us and shake the rafters.

Earle says, "The first Ferrari I had was a 1958 250 GT Berlinetta and Chris and I drove it to Arizona because our girlfriends were going to school there. The drive through the desert at night was worth the trip."

He owned the 1957 250 Testa Rossa that was the granddaddy of all TRs, a car with the ominous serial number 666.

Steve Earle drives the Ferrari 412 MI at the inaugural Monterey Historic Automobile Races (above). Below are the 250 GTOs of Earle and Chris Cord in 1974.

Earle, Cord, and other friends, such as Dick Messer (who now heads the Petersen Automotive Museum in Los Angeles), drove the TR and other cars out to Willow Springs Raceway and snuck onto the track. "We went out through Mint Canyon. At the track, we'd hold the chain up, drive under, and go like the wind. There was nobody out there, so we'd flog around. We'd been doing that since we were 16 years old, as soon as we could drive."

In 1969, Earle and Cord campaigned the Ferrari 612 Can-Am car throughout North America.

What does Earle consider the ultimate

❖ **"The thing I remember most,** *is that when Phil was going around Riverside in the 412 MI and you were standing in the pits, you could hear that car around the whole track."* — Steve Earle

Ferrari race car? The 1958 412 MI, in which Ferrari installed a special V-12 in a 335 S chassis. Maranello needed a hot rod to compete against the new Chevrolet V-8-powered specials, especially the beautiful new Scarabs. In the first *Los Angeles Times* Grand Prix at Riverside International Raceway in California, Phil Hill raced the 412 MI against the highly regarded Chuck Daigh in the Scarab.

"The thing I remember most," Earle explains, "is that when Phil was going around Riverside in the 412 MI and you were standing in the pits, you could hear that car around the whole track. It's hard to imagine, but it was so loud compared to everything else. And the sound was so different you could hear Phil when he got to turn six and was changing down, when he'd go around seven and up to eight and then down the straight. You thought, 'Oh my God! This is the most amazing car in the world.'

"They had one hell of a race, changing the lead a couple of times a lap until the Ferrari dropped out."

Though Earle has seen countless races in his life, he declares that event, "probably the only real race I ever saw. When did you ever see two guys purely duking it out?"

Earle would one day own the 412 MI and use it in his first vintage car races at Laguna Seca. What was it like to drive?

"It depended on the circuit. At Laguna Seca it was a pig—not a lot of fun. I always said that at Laguna the car felt like it had a waterbed in the back. When I went to Watkins Glen it was a totally different car because that's all high speed and that's what it was meant to do. It was never designed to race on a short, tight circuit. If Riverside were still around and you could have a vintage race there it would be one thing, but to run it at Laguna. . .

There are guys who want to reenact the match race between the Scarab and the 412 MI, but there's no way the 412 would get near it."

As a long-time Ferrari owner, Earle remembers what it was like to take delivery of your new car at Maranello decades ago.

"You'd go to the factory and get the car and put some gas in it and ask, 'Okay, now what are these switches for?' and they'd say, 'I don't know. Switch them and see what happens.'

"What about this one?'

"'Try it out and see what it does.'

"Then you'd get a ride with a road test driver in whatever he was going out in. They'd take you to Mr. Ferrari's office and you'd meet him—at least I did because Mr. Doheny, Chris Cord's dad, had a letter sent to introduce me.

"It was pretty magical. You'd go through the factory and you'd see them building the cars. Then you'd get in the car and drive it back to the hotel and try to go to sleep knowing it's sitting down in the garage."

What does Earle miss about those early Ferrari days?

"You know what was magic? The valvetrain noise, which we don't have anymore. You'd hear one coming down the road and you'd think, 'Oh my God, it's a Ferrari.'" **F**

Chic Vandagriff of Hollywood Sport Cars and Chuck Queener were part of the Earle-Cord Racing Ferrari West crew seen here with the Can-Am car at Donneybrook Raceway, Brainerd, Minnesota in 1970. Jim Adams qualified sixth and finished fourth.

New Zealand driver Chris Amon (above) was on the Ferrari factory team and campaigned Maranello's 612 Can-Am car during the 1969 season. Here he is at Watkins Glen ahead of former Ferrari driver John Surtees in a Chaparral-entered McLaren M12. Amon finished third. In designing the 6.2-liter V-12 for the Can-Am car (right), engineers used many of the principles from Ferrari's Formula 1 engines, creating the biggest powerplant Maranello had produced.

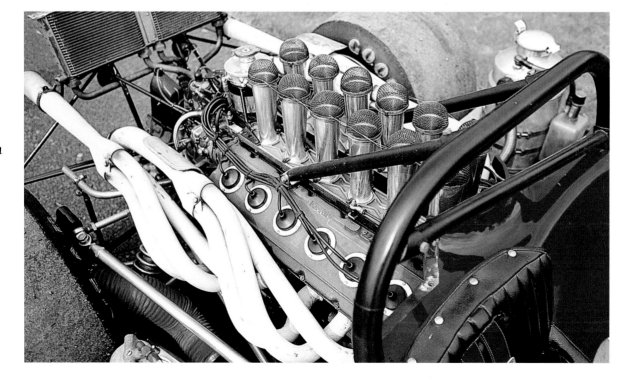

Ferrari's 612 Can-Am car (above) was raced through the 1971 season with V-12s that ranged from 5.0 to 6.9 liters. Later engines displaced 5.0 liters. In the last two years it was driven by little-known Jim Adams. Steve Earle, co-owner of the car then, remembers, "We went to Donnybrooke and Jim finished fourth overall. Chris Amon was driving the March that year and he came and looked at the car and told me, 'You know, I don't know anything about this guy who is driving the car, but he goes fast where we go fast.' And he was referring to guys like himself and Denny Hulme. Through the big sweepers at the end Jim was flat on it and flying."

When Porsche announced it would build 25 917s to meet the rules for 5.0-liter sports racing cars in 1970, Ferrari had to react quickly to counter the German threat. It committed to a like number of 512s and used lessons learned with the Can-Am cars for the new race car (below). While quick, the 512s were never a great threat to the 917s; Porsche won the manufacturers' crown in 1970 and 1971. Before Steve Earle and Chris Cord got the Can-Am Ferrari seen above, they owned a 512. When it was apparent it wasn't a Can-Am contender, they sold it to Roger Penske and Kirk F. White. Penske's race shop did its usual superb job of preparing the Ferrari, but with little success other than a third at Daytona. After the car dropped out at Le Mans, a Penske team member shook his head and said, "Ferraris are just different...." The ex-Penske 512 M is one of many still being used for vintage auto events and is seen below at the 2004 Rolex Monterey Historic Automobile Races.

Grand Prix

GRAND PRIX
A winning transition

AS WITH THE SPORTS CARS, FERRARI HAD TO MAKE THE SWITCH TO MID-MOUNTED engines, so 1960 was a transitional year, the team using the old front-engine 246s while American driver and testing wiz Richie Ginther experimented with a mid-engine machine. Ferrari won one race that year, the Italian Grand Prix, where Phil Hill took the last victory by a front-engine Grand Prix car.

There was a new formula for 1961, 1.5-liter engines, and the Carlo Chiti-designed mid-engine 156 was excellent. Phil Hill drove one to a World Driver's Championship.

Previous pages: Phil Hill in the Nürburgring's famous Karussel corner during the 1961 German Grand Prix. Right, Hill in the 1.5-liter mid-engine Ferrari Dino 156 during his season-long points battle with teammate Wolfgang von Trips. Hill figures his most frustrating race of the season was the French GP (right). "I was very upset after that race because I made the biggest screw-up of the entire season. Things could have been entirely different. I threw away nine points."

By contrast, 1962 was dismal, with no wins and Ferrari's race team went through a changing of the guard. This made 1963 another transitional year, marking the beginning of the cars created by the man who would do so much for Ferrari for many years: Mauro Forghieri. Success from his work came quickly, with John Surtees winning the 1964 driver's championship and Ferrari the constructors' title with the 158 F1.

This proved to be the pinnacle of Ferrari's Formula 1 success in the 1960s. The formula went to 3.0 liters in 1966, and the team won only three more races the rest of the decade, John Surtees at Monaco in 1966, Ludovico Scarfiotti in Italy the same year, and Jacky Ickx in the French Grand Prix in 1968.

The 1970s would be much better. ▣

• Phil Hill and the 1961 Grand Prix Season

World Driving Champion, 1961
Santa Monica, Calif.

At the Dutch GP, Hill's 156 F1 "sharknose" began to oversteer, making matters uncomfortable.

ONLY TWO U.S. DRIVERS HAVE WON THE FORMULA 1 DRIVER'S CHAMPIONSHIP: PHIL HILL AND MARIO Andretti. Hill's championship came in a Ferrari in 1961, Andretti's 16 years later driving for Team Lotus.

The circumstances of their title-winning races have an eerie similarity. Both drivers staged a season-long battle with their teammates for the championship—Hill versus German Count Wolfgang von Trips, and Andretti versus Swedish driver Ronnie Peterson. Each American would win his crown at the Italian Grand Prix at Monza, near Milan, and in both cases their teammates would die as the result of racing accidents at Monza.

Tragic symmetry.

Hill grew up in Santa Monica, California, began racing after World War II, and very quickly established himself as one

✦ ***"What I remember about the race*** *was the frustration of busting my ass and not being able to catch Moss."*—Phil Hill

future World Driving Champion had his first Grand Prix start in Jo Bonnier's Maserati 250F at Reims in 1958 on a grid that also included Americans Carroll Shelby and Troy Ruttman.

Hill's had his first factory Ferrari open-wheel ride at the Nürburgring in 1958 in a combined Formula 1/Formula 2 event, driving one of the F2 machines in a race that underlined the inherent dangers in racing back then. In just a 15-month period, four men who had been team drivers were killed: Luigi Musso, Alfonso "Fon" de Portago, Peter Collins, and Jean Behra.

Hill's debut open-wheel race for Ferrari was the event in which his friend Collins was killed. This led to Hill's seat on the Formula 1 team for 1959 and 1960, peaking with his win at the 1960 Italian GP, the last win ever scored by a front-engine Grand Prix car.

In his award-winning book about his sports car racing career, *Ferrari: A Champion's View*, Hill explained that deadly era: "It sounds cold, thinking about it now....They were all good friends. We were very defensive about anybody delving into the life or death aspects of racing. We tried to avoid it and not talk about it. In retrospect, I'm pretty certain we knew it was a losing discussion. We would

Carlo Chiti, the engineer behind the great Ferrari designs of 1961, Hill's championship year.

Ing. Vittorio Jano and Hill: Modena July 31, 1962.

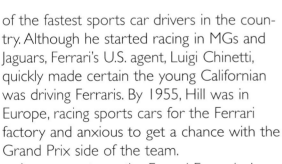

of the fastest sports car drivers in the country. Although he started racing in MGs and Jaguars, Ferrari's U.S. agent, Luigi Chinetti, quickly made certain the young Californian was driving Ferraris. By 1955, Hill was in Europe, racing sports cars for the Ferrari factory and anxious to get a chance with the Grand Prix side of the team.

As now, seats on the Ferrari Formula 1 team were few, and by 1958 Hill didn't have the reputation or other means to promote such a spot. Impatient to prove his worth, the

have had a tough time rationalizing why it was okay to continue. In that atmosphere, a lot of things that don't make any sense now were logical."

Then came 1961, the new 1.5-liter engine formula, and Ferrari's move, at last, to mid-engine F1 cars. At the Monaco Grand Prix on May 14, Stirling Moss finished first, Richie Ginther second, and Hill finished on the podium with a third-place finish. He was followed by Wolfgang von Trips in fourth.

Ginther took the lead at the start, Moss passed him on lap 14, and led until the end despite attempts first by Hill, then Ginther, to catch him. The Ferraris had the power, but Moss's car was lighter and more nimble. "I always liked Monaco," Hill explains, "the whole beachy atmosphere." But for the 1961 race, "Monaco was tough because Von Trips and I had been inactive all winter long. Richie in that prototype car with the 120-degree engine (a car he had tested off season) had an advantage on us. It wasn't enjoyable.

"What I remember about the race was the frustration of busting my ass and not being able to catch Moss. Richie had driven a 2.5-liter rear-engine car there the year before, and was faster in 1961. I kept trying to get him to pass me. Every so often I'd slow down and wave him past, but he wouldn't do it until the 75th lap. I don't know why."

The Dutch GP saw Jimmy Clark's Lotus 21 and Phil Hill's Ferrari 156 duel closely with Hill finishing ahead of Clark but behind Von Trips.

I figured he should have a go at Moss.

"Although this was a frustrating race, we had a look at our car's potential, which was promising, considering the Ferraris would be better suited to upcoming tracks." Point total: Hill 4 points, Von Trips 3 points.

Hill performed better at the Dutch Grand Prix in Zandvoort on May 22, finishing second behind Von Trips and ahead of third-place Jimmy Clark and fourth-place Moss. Hill and Von Trips had identical qualifying times, and Von Trips led from the start, while Hill fought a race-long duel with Clark. "I liked Zandvoort, the place, but it seemed our cars were always awkward there. It was a pleasant surprise to find that in 1961 we were as good as the rest, if not better. We had a chance to use the Ferrari's power for the first time, but I was annoyed that I had missed on the handling set up and should have added more understeer. After my tires got hot from a few laps of frantic driving, I was all arms and elbows, which is not the way you'd like it at Zandvoort, where a gentle understeer is preferable. Von Trips did a better job of it here than I did. He liked to shy away from oversteer, but I thought I had the hot setup and I was wrong.

"I spent most of the race fighting it out with Jimmy Clark, and remember being astounded at the way he could be almost anywhere, even off-line in the Lotus. This was before the polished Jimmy Clark we all remember so well. He could be out in the middle of the road, while if we made that much of a mistake in the Ferraris, we'd be off in a field. It was the first time we really saw the Clark/Lotus abilities, and, of course, there's nothing that breeds a wonderful driver like a wonderful car and Clark became a wonderful driver." Point total: Von Trips 12, Hill 10.

Things improved even more at the Belgian Grand Prix in Spa on June 18, where Hill topped the podium, beating second-place Von Trips, third-place Ginther, and fourth-place finisher Olivier Gendebien. After a brief leading spurt by Gendebien, Hill took the lead and controlled the race until the finish. "I liked the track very much because it was fast and took great precision. It was very rewarding to be able to put together a great lap at Spa. I had only been there three or four times before. [The track's] located in the Ardennes Forest, the same forest as the Nürburgring, just across the border in

Germany. It was as beautiful as it was challenging." Point total: Hill 19, Von Trips 18.

Ask Hill now about his relationship with Von Trips, and he'll pause a long time before answering. We're all thrown into situations in which we end up working with people who otherwise might not be our friends. There was a natural gap between the mechanic whose first racing loves were midgets running on dusty California race tracks, and a titled German count who began racing in a Porsche. Friends? Yes. Pals? No. "Anyone as intense as I was at that time was a bit skeptical of those like Von Trips who seemed, at least on the surface, a bit lackadaisical."

Things went downhill at the French Grand Prix in Rheims on July 2, where Giancarlo Baghetti finished first, Dan Gurney second, Clark third, and Innes Ireland fourth. The Ferraris had the front row, but newcomer Baghetti won after Von Trips and Ginther dropped out and Hill dropped back. He explains: "I was very upset after that race because I made the biggest screw-up of the entire season. Things could have been entirely different. I threw away nine points. Everybody was getting stones through their radiator (which put Ginther and Von Trips out), and I'd managed to avoid following other cars at

❖ "Trips was always capable of taking greater risks than I was willing to. He had a capacity to go to the edge and beyond it." — Phil Hill

high speed to prevent that same problem. I was about to lap Moss and I thought, 'I've got to get by Moss before we get to (the slow) Thillois (corner) or he'll put a stone through my radiator.' I passed Moss, but I spun and he T-boned me in the middle of the spin.

"I'd become a master at taking a chance at Thillois, a spin meaning I'd just get into a lower gear, do an on-the-gravel spin and drive off. They never even knew in the pits that I'd done it, because it only took a few seconds. But Moss and I collided, and although we had on-board starters that year, the batteries had been cooked dry. The car was drivable—I finished ninth—but I had to push start it to get going again… and it's an uphill push. It took laps and laps, and when the car did start it ran over my foot.

"I found that the best thing was to not try to start it by pushing, jumping in, sticking it into gear, and letting the clutch in, because by then the car would have stopped. (This all must sound very foreign to a modern Grand Prix driver.) Finally I reached in while the car was moving and yanked it into gear and had to chase the car to jump in. In the process it

Phil Hill's main rival for the 1961 crown was German Count Wolfgang von Trips. Here Trips is turning for the well-known La Source hairpin on Belgium's quick Spa circuit.

ran over my Achilles tendon. That smarted." Point total: Hill 19, Von Trips 18.

Both Von Trips and Hill were back in form at the British Grand Prix at Aintree on July 15, with Von Trips first, Hill second, Ginther third, and Jack Brabham fourth. It was a three-Ferrari front row, and they finished one-two-three, but after much drama. "I hated Aintree," Hill recalls, "because it rained so hard and it was difficult to predict where the puddles would be. I had one really bad moment in the middle of the race where I almost collected the gate post at Melling Crossing, and it took the steam out of me (Moss spun and Henry Taylor crashed heavily at the same place). I had earned a reputation as a rain driver, but I'd already put that aside earlier in the season at the Nürburgring, where I was leading in the sports car race, but flew off the road in a big way. Now I was just happy to come away from Aintree with six points and my life." Point total: Von Trips 27, Hill 25.

By now, the points race was becoming a heavy weight to carry. Hill: "It began pretty early from the public, team management, the press, and myself, but I never heard one word about it from Enzo Ferrari, who probably figured it would be a jinx or something. This was the year SEFAC (a French financial com-

bine that bought a portion of Ferrari as a means of injecting needed capital) was formed and we had big French tycoons in the pits. One of them was always trying to make me or Von Trips the favorite, and that became very awkward and unpleasant."

And there was the pressure from his teammate: "Von Trips was always capable of taking greater risks than I was willing to, and I was anxious about the degree to which I would have go to do battle with him. He had a capacity to go to the edge and beyond it. Remember, he already had the name 'Von Crash.' In my first Formula 1 race with Ferrari at Monza in 1958, Von Trips ran up the back of Harry Schell and took them both off the road at the Curva Grande, and you just don't run into the back of anybody going into the Curva Grande. He also took out the lead Formula 2 cars at Monte Carlo the year before by screwing up at St. Devote."

Von Trips extended his lead at the German Grand Prix, held at the Nürburgring on August 6. Moss finished first, Von Trips second, Hill third, and Clark fourth. Hill won pole with the first-ever sub-9 minute lap of the hilly, twisting 14-mile circuit, 10.3 seconds faster than Von Trips, who finished on the second row. Moss led from the start, while Hill and Von Trips dueled much of the race, but as they finished, they came into a sudden rainstorm just short of the finish. Recalls Hill: "We were both all over the road, and damn lucky we didn't take each other out. Von Trips managed to get things gathered up fractionally ahead of me and beat me to the line by a nose.

"I hated having to practice on one setup and race on another. We'd set up the cars for the new Dunlop high-hysteresis tires—it was wet—but just before the start it began to dry. Dunlop demanded we change tires, figuring they'd never last on a dry track with our amount of negative camber. Moss, in the light Lotus, used the tires against Dunlop's dictates, and came in on the cords, but he won.

"I was also bothered by the fact I'd had that record qualifying time, but was not able to repeat that effort in the race. Perhaps I'd begun to realize that I had had a better racing year in 1960, when the relative quality of the car kept me in the middle of the pack, and 1961 was not, in my mind, going all that well." Point total: Von Trips 33, Hill 29.

One thing most automotive enthusiasts

Phil Hill is all smiles after winning the Belgian Grand Prix at Spa.

don't realize about Hill is that long before the racing and now, long after, he has been fascinated with things mechanical. Big things, like Packards and Pierce-Arrows, but also their smallest component parts. Large clutch plates and tiny springs. Heavy engine blocks and light carburetor floats. I've seen him fascinated by an oddball pre-World War I carburetor, examining it though several pairs of dime store reading glasses run out on his nose to get just the right magnification to reveal the holes and crannies.

This concern with things mechanical would serve Hill well at Monza in September, and may be one reason he came away the champion.

"Monza was frustrating from the first day of practice. The year before I won the race hands down, but this year everything seemed to go wrong. Tell me a race in 1961 where things went right?

"I never had the satisfaction of feeling I had driven a race right all through the season. I didn't feel I was making as good a use of what was available as I should.

"Then, the first day of practice at Monza, I had this crazy gear selection problem. It would go first-second, but when I went to third it would go back to first and second, and it wasn't until I got over to the shift linkage's last track that I could get into third or fourth. Worse yet, no one would believe me. We wasted a good 45 minutes or an hour before they would get on with it. I finally had to have the mechanic get in the car and drive around the paddock to convince them. I was throwing fits.

"Then, I was losing 1.5 seconds a lap just on the banking. I was back on the second row, and Monza was my track. I held the lap record there several times. Obviously the engine was off because I was losing time on the banking where the driver has nothing to do with the lap time. We should all be the same in that stretch.

"At first, they weren't going to change the engine. This was also the time I was trying to get them to change the lip on the windscreen and Ferrari, who hated to have anyone criticize his cars, asked me something like, 'Are you sure it isn't your right foot?' (Sound familiar to anyone who has seen the movie *Grand Prix*?)

"During the week before practice, my car was the one that had been brought up to Monza for testing, so it had a bit more mileage on it than the others. As for the engines, we had already damaged the valve springs. We found that our tires were heating up on the inside edge (remember, they had that very visible negative camber) and Dunlop demanded we take some of the camber out of the rear wheels. We did that and gained a lot of speed down the straightaway, which took the engine right up into its 'break-the-valve-springs' range—9700-9800 rpm—which we'd had a bit of at Spa. Naturally Ferrari changed the back axle ratio, but in those few laps of high rpm, the damage had been done. The rest of the team went out of the race with engine failure except, of course, for Von Trips.

"My car had obviously come back to Monza without an engine change, so I assumed it already had some broken valve springs. Once those little inner springs were broken you couldn't hear anything wrong when you revved the engine, but it was only a matter of a short time until they failed.

"At any rate, I insisted my engine be changed for the race. We stayed at a small country hotel, and knowing the little things that can go wrong in an engine swap—such as throttles not right when carburetors have to be quickly changed from one engine to the next—I was up at 6 the next morning to drive the car, to run things in a bit and try some standing starts."

"Right from the start of the race, I knew the engine had been the problem, because the car was its old self. I was leading before the end of the first lap, only to come around on the second and find waving yellow flags, debris and an upside-down Ferrari at the Parabolica.

"How did I react? I didn't know whose car it was until I came around and Von Trips' number was missing from the pit sign. And then I didn't dwell on it. I'd seen so many accidents in which the car was wrapped up like a pretzel and the driver had walked away. As the race progressed, I had other worries, watching my teammates disappear one-by-one from the list, wondering if their engines had failed and if mine would be next. I was walking on eggshells, trying to win at the slowest possible speed and being as gentle as I could with the engine.

Opening laps of the 1961 Italian Grand Prix with the four Ferrari team cars on Monza's banking. Phil Hill, the future champion, leads Richie Ginther, Ricardo Rodriguez, and Wolfgang von Trips, who would soon suffer his fatal accident.

"When the race was over, the first thing I asked Chiti when I got to the pits was, 'How is Von Trips?' I knew in an instant just from the look on Carlo's face that Von Trips was dead, though he never said it to me, and just wanted me to get up to the winner's stand to enjoy the victory."

That would never really happen. Obviously there was no party that evening, and in the morning Hill's happy feelings, almost disbelief, that he'd won the championship were countered by Von Trips' death. And there was the funeral to attend, including the long, slow walk from Von Trips' castle to the cemetery. In the end, there never really was a celebration.

"It may sound foolish now, but somehow I felt too involved in the death of Von Trips. I wasn't, of course, and was just another driver of another car. What I probably felt was that

with all the lauding there should also be some kind of guilt over it. I probably felt that it was appropriate to feel this guilt and not be bold and say, 'Well, he screwed up.'"

Under the 1961 rules, a driver could only count the results from his five best finishes during the 8-race season. Von Trips' total stayed at 33. After dropping the 4 points for the third-place at the Nürburgring and adding the 9 for Monza, Hill's added to 34, making him the 1961 World Champion.

The U.S. Grand Prix was held on October 8, but without any Ferraris. The Italian company had already won the constructors' championship, and Hill the drivers' crown, so the cars were kept in Maranello. "I was thoroughly annoyed and disappointed to not have the car there. But it wasn't totally unexpected, because Ferrari was weird about things like that, pulling the rug out from underneath you, canceling things and changing his mind. It was also embarrassing, because you should be able to go to your own home race, and to have to spend my time riding around in the back of convertibles made me feel very awkward."

"I'm also very disappointed," Hill adds, "that all those first mid-engine Ferrari F1 cars were destroyed by the factory."

Hill did another season with Ferrari before quitting to race for the new ATS team with his former Ferrari team manager, Carlo Chiti. It was, at best, an unpleasant year and I remember the time we were at Donington's famous museum of Grand Prix cars, rounded a corner, and there was an ATS GP car. Our friend, Doug Nye, said, "Well, Phil, what do you think of this car?"

The driver just stared past the ATS and said, with only a little grin on his face, "What car? I don't see any car."

Though he moved to the Cooper team for 1964, it was no better, and these days Hill wonders about his real motivations in signing with those two second-rate teams. After a few more one-off rides, Hill's Formula 1 career ended.

The sports car racing continued and he finished his career with Jim Hall's Chaparral team, having the unique honor of winning his last race, the 1967 BOAC 6 Hours at Brands Hatch, co-driving a Chaparral 2F with Mike Spence and happy to have defeated Jackie Stewart and Chris Amon in a Ferrari 330 P4. ◨

Decades after the tragic day at Monza, Phil Hill visited Wolfgang von Trips' grave in Germany.

*The United States'
two Formula 1
World Champions:
Phil Hill (left) and
Mario Andretti.*

• John Surtees MBE on Leaving Ferrari

World Driving Champion, 1964
Edenbridge, Kent, Great Britain

Surtees leads the 1000 km at the Nürburgring in 1964. The 275 P lost a wheel and finished 46th.

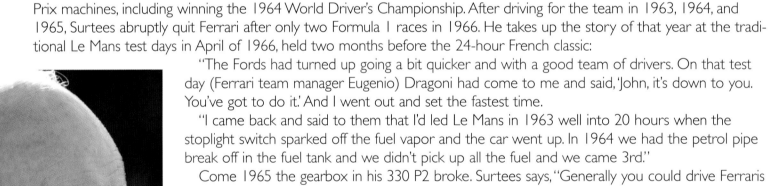

JOHN SURTEES BROUGHT FERRARI A GREAT DEAL OF GLORY IN BOTH SPORTS RACING CARS AND GRAND Prix machines, including winning the 1964 World Driver's Championship. After driving for the team in 1963, 1964, and 1965, Surtees abruptly quit Ferrari after only two Formula 1 races in 1966. He takes up the story of that year at the traditional Le Mans test days in April of 1966, held two months before the 24-hour French classic:

"The Fords had turned up going a bit quicker and with a good team of drivers. On that test day (Ferrari team manager Eugenio) Dragoni had come to me and said, 'John, it's down to you. You've got to do it.' And I went out and set the fastest time.

"I came back and said to them that I'd led Le Mans in 1963 well into 20 hours when the stoplight switch sparked off the fuel vapor and the car went up. In 1964 we had the petrol pipe break off in the fuel tank and we didn't pick up all the fuel and we came 3rd."

Come 1965 the gearbox in his 330 P2 broke. Surtees says, "Generally you could drive Ferrari very nearly at maximum, so I said there's only one way we will beat these people [in 1966]. That is, we will have to go along and be the hare. People like Dan Gurney are not going to just allow me to disappear. I'll go bang from the start and with a bit of luck I hope the car will last. Mechanically it's more likely to last than the Fords if we set the right pace from the start and the other two Ferraris can run a slightly reduced speed. And that was the strategy."

Prior to the Le Mans race in June, Surtees had been practicing for the upcoming Grand Prix season, while simultaneously recuperating from a bad sports car accident in Canada the previous autumn.

"I had a 1965 Grand Prix car and they put a 2.4-liter V-6 engine in it for me to do the Tasman Series in 1965, but I had my accident, which ruled out doing the Tasman races (held in New Zealand and Australia from January to March). But the car was there and it was the only car available for me to do my convalescence once I started walking again. So I went round and round the Modena circuit in this car and set the fastest times we'd ever set there. The car was very quick.

"And then they wheeled out the new 3.0-liter (V-12), which was supposed to have 320 horsepower, but it was 150 pounds overweight and had, in fact, 290 horsepower. I was about

2.5 seconds a lap slower than I was in the 2.4."

Surtees would have preferred to race the older V-6 car in the first event as it was more suited to the tight, twisty Monaco Grand Prix circuit, "but Dragoni came up and said, 'We've made a 12-cylinder and we can't have our team leader in a V-6.'

"I said, 'Aren't we here to race?'"

But Surtees consented, saying, "'Alright, I doubt whether I'll finish. We know very well we can drive the car hard, but the gearbox is a bit questionable, and, you know? That happened. I led the race until the gearbox failed. Hard work because (Jackie) Stewart was behind me and (Lorenzo) Bandini in the (Ferrari 2.4) V-6 was behind him. That was a race just thrown away."

Bandini not only finished second, but set fastest lap in the car Surtees would have rather driven, "So I was unhappy about that."

Next race was the Belgian Grand Prix on the very fast Spa circuit and the V-12 car was better because, "Rocchi had come up with a revised cylinder head, which gave the engine just under 320 horsepower. It was much better and I put the car on pole and led the race, but then the heavens opened up. Jochen Rindt in the Cooper-Maserati went by and I decided to follow for a few laps before passing him and winning the race (by 42 seconds).

"Dragoni was upset because I'd allowed a Maserati (Ferrari's cross-town Modenese rival) to be in front and I said, 'Well, I drove the race to win with the tires I had.' I didn't have as good an aquaplaning situation as the Cooper, and I said it is far better for me to follow in his path and then go as I did and disappear when I wanted.

"Dragoni didn't even congratulate me for winning the race.

"Then we get to Le Mans and they tell me there's a change of plans. You're not starting. Mr. Agnelli [Giovanni Agnelli, head of Fiat] is coming and they want Bandini, an Italian, to start in the car.

"I said, 'It's silly. What are we doing? Are we here to win races or are we here to play games? If you want to play games, do it with someone else.'

"So I want back to Maranello and we had our divorce… which lost me probably a couple of World Championships."

Years later, not long before Enzo Ferrari died, Surtees spoke with him. Surtees recalls:

♦ **"The old man said,**
'Remember the good times, John, and not the mistakes.'" — *John Surtees*

"The Old Man said, 'Remember the good times, John, and not the mistakes.'
"That's life." **F**

Surtees in the 158 F1 at the non-championship event at Solitude.

Below, 1964, Giulio Borsari congratulates Surtees after his victory in the German Grand Prix on the 14-mile Nürburgring.

The 1970s

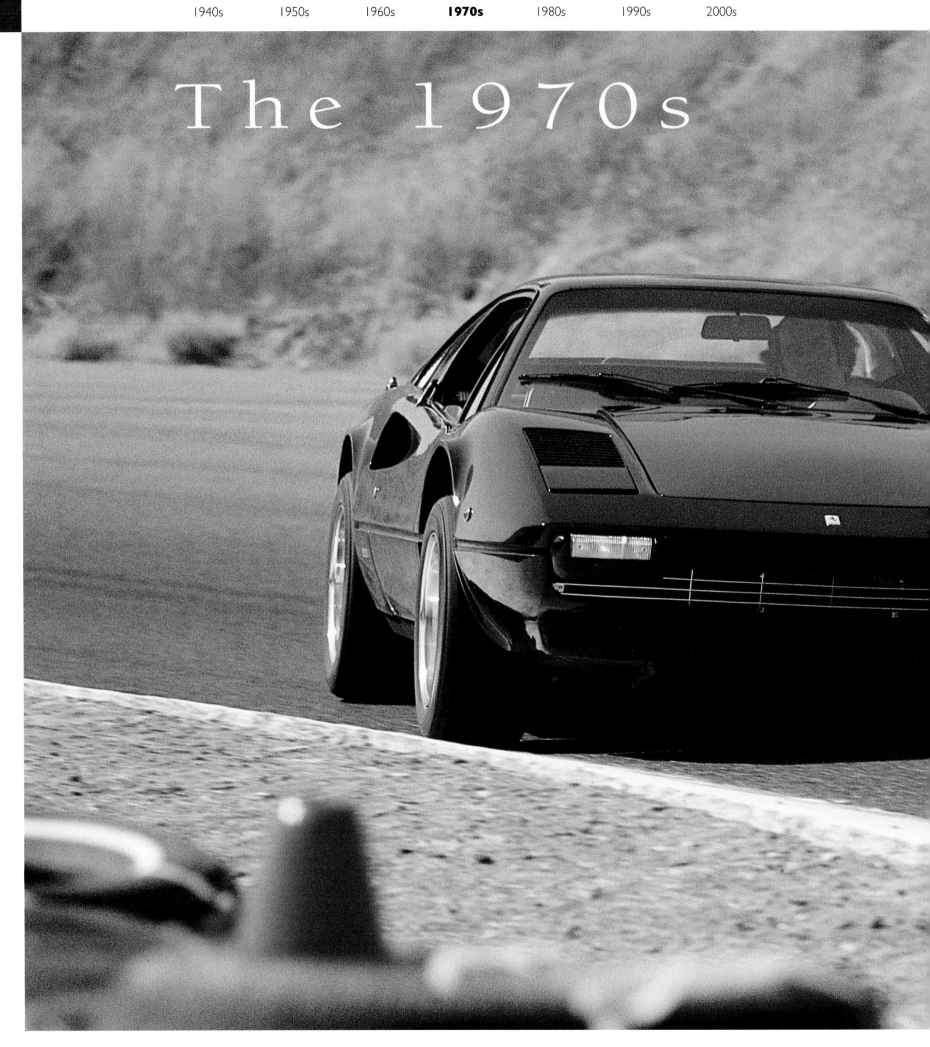

The 1970s

Previous pages: Bob Bondurant drifts a Ferrari 308 at Sears Point Raceway. Ferrari's 365 GTB/4 (below) wasn't officially called a Daytona, but inherited the nickname. The car's distinctive shape was penned by young Leonardo Fioravanti at Pininfarina.

PRODUCTION CARS
Creating modern classics

FERRARI BEGAN THE 1970S DECADE WITH THE 365 GTB/4 DAYTONA, BUT LIKE ALL automakers it was headed for difficult times. Car companies had to face new safety and emissions regulations that were toughest in the critical U.S. market, but varied from country to country. Then along came two fuel "shocks," one in 1973, the second in 1979, disrupting much of the motoring world.

In 1970, the Dino was upgraded to the very popular 246 GT, followed by the GTS, which had a removable hardtop. The next year brought the ungainly looking and short-lived 365 GTC/4.

By contrast, the following new model from Maranello stayed in production for 17 years, the big, handsome, and comfortable 365 GT/4 2+2. It became the 400 GT in 1976—the first Ferrari with an automatic transmission—and the 412 in 1985.

While Pininfarina had been designing all the Ferrari production cars for many years, Bertone was given a shot at the next version of the "small" Ferrari. Powered by a mid-engine, transverse 3.0-liter V-8, the car was called a Dino early on and had 2+2 seating. To some the styling was too wedge-like, but this 308 GT4 was a good seller for Ferrari… and Bertone's last car for Maranello.

In the early 1970s, exotic car makers were expected to have a big mid-engine machine: hence the DeTomaso Pantera and Lamborghini Countach. Ferrari gave in as of the 1971 Turin Auto Show with the Pininfarina 365 GT/4 Berlinetta Boxer concept. Finally reaching production in 1974, the car had a mid-engine flat-12 that was mounted above the transmission and started at 4.4 liters, going to 5.0 in 1976. A highly regarded car, the Boxer was in production for 11 years.

Another long-lived Ferrari made its debut in 1975 as the 308 GTB, which had a transverse 3.0-liter V-8 behind the cockpit. Two years later, a removable-top GTS version went on sale. The car became the 3.2-liter 328 in 1985 and stayed in production until 1989.

While the era of special coach-built cars for wealthy owners was over, Pininfarina wowed the world with one of the most outrageous concept cars ever, the 512 S-based Modulo. **F**

At Pininfarina's research and design center outside Torino, Italy, the breathtaking Ferrari 512 S-based 1970 Modulo concept car is displayed next to the Mythos from 1989. Pininfarina points out the double-shell form of the car's profile and the unique wheel arch treatments. To enable the driver and passenger to get into the Modulo, the entire cockpit surround slides forward.

The 1971 Ferrari 365 GTC/4... not Pininfarina's most successful design. This was an era when all automakers were struggling to meet new bumper and lighting rules, not always with the best results. The GTC/4 had a short lifespan.

La Ferrari costruisce in piccola serie motori a 12 cilindri dal 1946 e le sue vere Granturismo compendiano le esperienze dirette di 25 anni di vittoriose affermazioni.

Depuis 1946 Ferrari construit en petite série des moteurs 12 cylindres et les voitures actuelles de Grandtourisme sont la panacée de 25 ans d'expériences victorieuses.

Ferrari have been manufacturing limited production 12 cylinder engines of various capacity since 1946 and their range of thoroughbred Granturismo cars incorporates the direct experiences of 25 years of unequalled racing successes.

A favorite Ferrari from the early 1970s was the 365 GTS/4, the Spider version of the Daytona. This model became so popular that after the Daytona went out of production body shops were decapitating the coupe versions to convert them into spiders.

In 1979, long after competition Daytonas were out of major contention, John Morton and Tony Adamowicz drove this version to a second overall in, appropriately, the 24-hour race at Daytona. The night before the race, team manager Otto Zipper died and the team almost withdrew the car. But Morton and Adamowicz soldiered on through the 24 hours in what was almost an antique. Porsche's turbocharged race cars proved rather fragile and the Ferrari quite robust, hanging tough to the end.

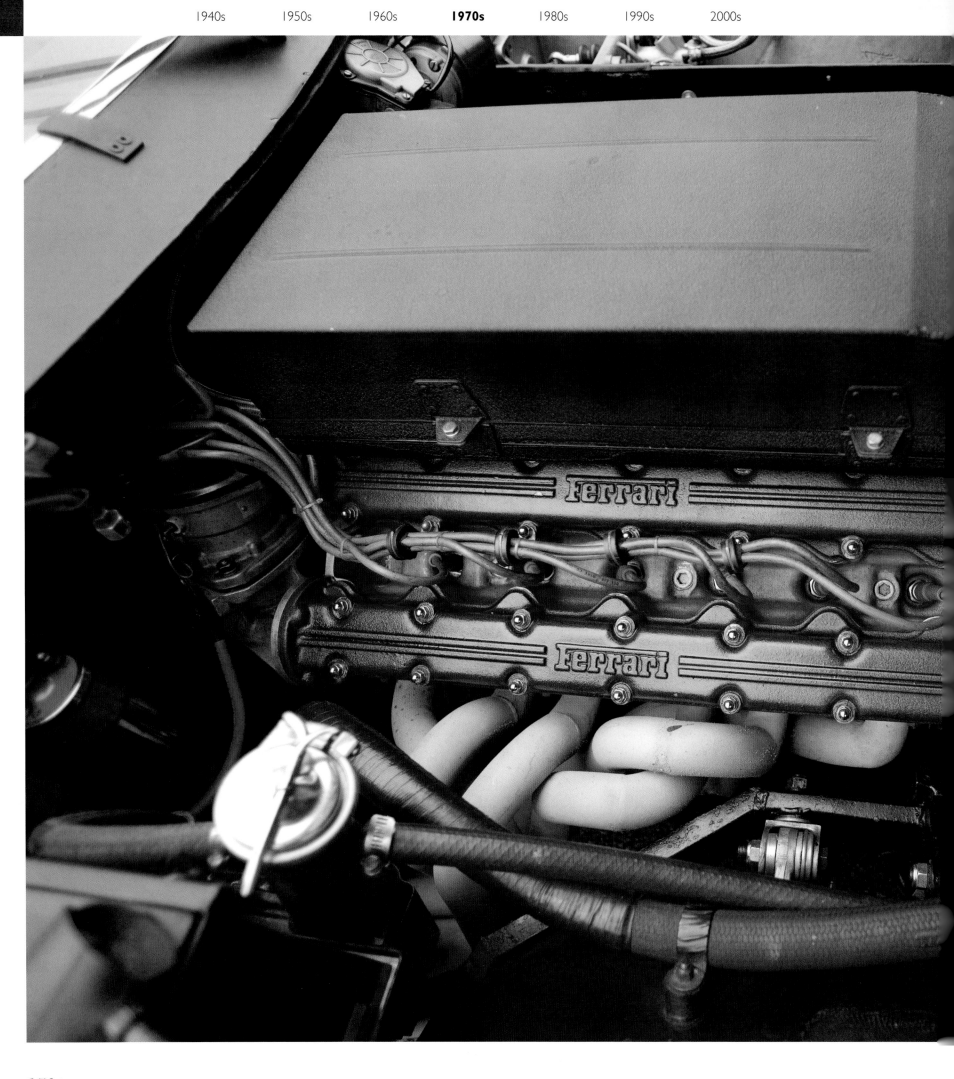

Under the hood of the Morton/Adamowicz Daytona (left), the V-12 with "Ferrari" cast in its camshaft covers, twisty white header pipes, and Weber carbs encased in a cool air box. Like so many Ferrari engines, this V-12 was as reliable as it was powerful. Above is the Daytona entered in the 1973 24 Hours of Le Mans by the French importer, Charles Pozzi. The car finished sixth overall and won its class.

• John Morton

Racing driver
Manhattan Beach, California

MICHAEL SCHUMACHER BROUGHT GLORY TO FERRARI THROUGHOUT THE GRAND PRIX WORLD. Maranello's sports racing cars have won on every continent in the world. And yet arguably the most legendary race for any Ferrari in the U.S. wasn't a win and it wasn't by a Formula 1 car, a Testa Rossa, or any other purebred racing Ferrari. Instead, the drive came in a model that wasn't originally meant to be a race car and it happened years later than it should, at a time when the car could have been in a museum.

In fact, John Morton, one of the two drivers of the car, says, "Ferrari Daytonas were never great race cars. They were heavy, a little under-tired, and just never developed to race. They had a fairly fragile transmission, though we never had that trouble. But the balance could change from a full to light fuel load and then the brakes would lock up and there was no way to compensate for that.

"It had a fair amount of power, but it was a big, heavy engine. It was easy to drive in the sense that it was a reliable engine like Ferraris are if they're put together right, but it wasn't all that fast."

Then he adds, "It was almost an antique."

Ferrari 365 GTB/4 Daytona with chassis number 16407 was finished in Maranello in time to be entered by Luigi Chinetti's North American Racing Team in the 1973 24 Hours of Le Mans. It was raced there for the next three years with no notable finishes and sold in 1977 to actor Robert Carradine. That's right, the guy who played Lewis Skolnick in the *Revenge of the Nerds* movies. Carradine raced the car for several years, teamed with Morton, but in 1979 the Daytona was sold to Bill Nicolas and Jim McRoberts.

The pair had no racing experience, but entered the car in the 1979 24 Pepsi Challenge, known familiarly as the 24 Hours of Daytona. First major car competition of the year, the race around the clock was held in early February.

Bruno Borri's Modena Sports Cars in Hollywood, one of the better garages in Los Angeles, prepped 16407 for Daytona. And they added a legend to the team who was the official entrant for the car.

Otto Zipper had been around the Southern California sports car scene for decades, owning Ferrari and Porsche dealerships. Like Luigi Chinetti, he was instrumental in getting young race drivers into important cars, men like Ken Miles. Now 64, Zipper was, Morton explains, "Kind of retired from racing, but this got him out of the house. It was a

John Morton in 1979 when he and Tony Adamowicz drove a Ferrari Daytona to second place in Daytona's 24-hour Pepsi Challenge.

holiday thing for him, but he was a good manager and took it very seriously."

Morton and his teammate, Tony Adamowicz—known as "Tony A-to-Z"—qualified the car a respectable 24th in the field of 67 race cars. Since 16407 had finished 10th in 1977 and 8th in 1978 at Daytona, it could be predicted they would finish in the top 20 in 1979.

The competition looked tough and was separated into three classes. Fastest were the GTX machines, which basically meant Porsches of several types, mainly 935 Turbos. GTO race cars included Porsches, the latest factory Ferrari 512 BB/LMs with their long Pininfarina-developed aero bodies, Camaros, and this old Daytona. Slowest were the GTU cars with still more Porsches, rotary-engine Mazdas, and a few Datsun Z-cars.

Ready to race on Saturday, 16407's team went to dinner Friday evening. Morton continues the story-"I asked Otto if he was going to join us and he said no, he wasn't feeling that well because he had a kidney stone and thought he might pass it that night. The next morning we got up and everybody was getting ready to go to the track.

"Sylvia (Morton's wife) and I were going to breakfast and the crew was just coming out of the restaurant and asked, 'Have you seen Otto?' We hadn't, they said he hadn't shown up for breakfast and they thought he hadn't gone to the track early. We got a maid to open his room and he was dead in bed."

Zipper had died of a heart attack during the night and, "Everyone was quite emotional about it, a very tough deal, and they wanted to withdraw the car. Tony and I wanted to run the Ferrari, not really to make a statement, but we thought it would be appropriate to race the car. Sylvia and Tony's girlfriend, Vicki, talked the team into running, thinking Otto would have wanted that, so we did. We put black tape diagonally across the hood of the car in honor of Otto.

"It was a shame he couldn't be there because we had an incredible performance, largely due to the Porsche Turbos being so fragile at the time, because we were obviously not competitive with the Porsches."

But certainly more durable. First the new Ferraris BB/LMs were withdrawn when problems with their Michelin tires caused two crashes and it wasn't prudent to continue. Then the Porsches' turbos began to fail and the venerable Ferrari began to creep up the field.

Morton recalls, "We didn't have a trouble-free run. We were burning up the inside edges of the tires and put the car in the garage and made a camber change, which was a big job. They were good mechanics and quick, but we lost quite a bit of time there. And then we had an oil leak and had to change an oil line later in the race.

"Our pit was not a Penske operation. Our fueling rig was a 55-gallon drum up on a stand and it dripped and they had rags around it. Sylvia timed the whole 24 hours without a rest and just the smell of the fuel all night long...."

Even though the Ferrari BB/LMs had been withdrawn, Luigi Chinetti stayed in the pits watching and at one point asked Morton, "What position are you in?"

"This was late at night, maybe not quite halfway, and I asked Sylvia. She told me we were seventh and I told him and he said, 'No!' I said, 'Yes, we're seventh,' and he said, 'No, not seventh,' like don't bother me with your bullshit. But we were seventh and we gradually worked our way up."

As the Porsche Turbos blew up, the Daytona edged toward the lead of the race. "We'd be fourth overall and then a Turbo would blow and we'd be third. . . .

"When we were well up, one of the Whittington brothers, with the boost screwed all the way up in the Turbo, passed me. They'd already blown about four of them and I thought, 'Please blow up again' and he blew another one. That cinched our second place."

It hadn't been easy. Morton tells that the Daytona was a physically difficult car to drive, "With exceptionally heavy steering. Tony and I got so tired we could only do one tank of fuel at a time, a little over an hour, before changing drivers. I remember being ushered back from the motorhome to the pits, it was a cold night and I'm soaking wet and thinking, 'I don't really want to get in this #&%@ car again.' And we had to do that over and over. At the end of the race I couldn't take my driving suit off because I was cramping all over."

Morton adds, "It was a real ordeal, one of those things that takes a lot out of you, but that makes it better.

"And we won the GTO category and were second overall. Had it had been Le Mans we would have been first overall because the winning car, the Interscope Porsche driven by Danny Ongais, Ted Field, and Hurley Haywood, broke and they just sat at the start/finish line for the last 15-20 minutes. At Le Mans you had to do the last lap in 400 percent of your qualifying time or something like that. At Daytona that would have been around 8 minutes and they parked for 15-20 and then started the thing up and putted across the line. They'd had a huge lead and did win by IMSA rules."

Morton, one of the United State's most versatile top-line drivers for decades, still occasionally thinks about the race in 1979, "Because of all the races I've run I have to rate that in the top few. I think it is the best a Daytona did in big, international competition. And it was a Ferrari Daytona at Daytona.

"I'd be the first to admit it was fluky, but we beat a lot of good cars and teams and we were just a put-together team run by a Ferrari repair shop in Hollywood. It was bittersweet because of Otto, but I had the feeling we had done something for him." F

Luigi Chinetti, above, and Bruno Borri pulled together after Zipper's death.

Below, Morton and Adamowicz trade places behind the wheel of "an antique."

You probably won't find many Ferrari fans with a passion for the 365/400/412 2+2 series, but these highly respected, comfortable, big machines can be found in many collections. Launched as the 365 GT/4 2+2 in 1972, it was powered by a 4.4-liter, 320-horsepower V-12. The engine was increased to 4.9 liters and 340 horsepower four years later, and the 400 Automatic became the first Ferrari with an automatic transmission. In 1985, the 2+2 became the 412. Not meant for cutting hot lap times, the big Ferrari 2+2s nevertheless shine as excellent touring machines.

While Pininfarina fulfilled it usual role as the designers of Ferraris with the 1975 308 GTB (left), Bertone was asked to create the shape of the 308 GT4. The 2+2 was launched in late 1973 with a transverse-mounted 250-horsepower V-8 behind the passenger cabin. In 1976, Bertone unveiled its Rainbow show car (below) based on a shortened GT4 chassis at the Turin Show.

At the 1971 Turin Motor Show, Ferrari showed its first big-horse-power mid-engine model, the 365 GT/4 Berlinetta Boxer, which went into production two years later. Designed by Pininfarina, the Boxer initially had a 4.4-liter, 380 horsepower flat-12 and a top speed of around 180 mph. Ferrari's second edition of the Boxer was the 5.0-liter 512 BB in 1976. Working to meet ever-tougher emissions regulations, Maranello adapted fuel injection to the flat-12 for 1981. Meeting these rules cut horsepower from the 365 Boxer's 380 to the 512 BB's 360 to the BBi's 340, though torque didn't suffer. Boxers were never official-ly sold in the U.S., but many were imported and certified as "gray market" cars.

• Ralph Lauren on Ferraris

Designer
New York, New York

"THE FIRST CAR I EVER BOUGHT WAS A MORGAN, AND I LOVED IT FOR YEARS," RALPH LAUREN REMINISCES. The man who is now one of the major arbiters in the world of fashion was just getting started at the time. "I lived in the Bronx and I drove my Morgan home and parked it on the street. I couldn't afford to put it in a garage."

Lauren established the Polo label in 1967, focusing on ties, but soon branched into men's clothing, adding women's styles in 1971. The guy who once couldn't afford to garage his Morgan was now able to raise his automotive sights.

"I got a Porsche and I was hooked," Lauren continues. "Then one day I came out of the Connaught Hotel in London and I saw this black convertible and said, 'What is that?'

"I had not been into Ferraris at that time and America had stopped making convertibles. Then I saw this black convertible with this beautiful shape… it was a Daytona Spider. It got me hooked. I got into the idea of it, though I didn't drive it."

Lauren didn't buy a Ferrari at that time, but that would soon change. "One day I was out in East Hampton with Jann Wenner of *Rolling Stone* magazine, who lived near me. He wanted to drive my Porsche Turbo and I wanted to see what his Ferrari was like. We took a long ride down the Montauk Highway and the sound of the Ferrari was so amazing that from that day on I was hooked on Ferraris. That was the beginning of my long relationship with the cars.

"The Daytona was the first Ferrari I got and I now have the good fortune of owning a few of them. And every one is a different experience. The sounds are all distinctive and each car is unique in its spirit and individuality. Whether it's a short-wheelbase Berlinetta, a 250 LM, or a GTO, they all offer different adventures.

"I fell in love with driving Ferraris and their spirit, but also their looks. Having a lot of cars and being able to drive different ones from Porsches to Aston Martins, there is a 'thorough-bredness' to the Ferraris that is unique, a breeding and heritage that is distinctive. They make you smile, and do the same for people who come over to see them."

Lauren doesn't like to pick a favorite Ferrari from his collection, but says, "I love the sensibility of the Testa Rossa in that it has all the racing elements and yet is very usable. I have a pontoon-fender TR that is totally drivable anywhere I want to take it. It feels like a race car."

✤ *"Then I saw this black convertible*
with this beautiful shape. . . it was a Daytona Spider.
It got me hooked."— Ralph Lauren

There is a logical comparison between two internationally famous firms that have flourished with strong, recognizable leaders, Ferrari under Enzo Ferrari and Luca di Montezemolo, and Polo under Ralph Lauren. The latter says, "Luca is a friend of mine. We got to know each other because I admire Ferraris and he admires Polo. He is a very exciting guy who is interested in absorbing what is around him and developing his business, but he also has a passion for the craft, for his art.

"I think there is a similarity in that we are passionate about what we do. At the same time, we've both taken something that was a distinct concept and broadened it into a thriving company. Ferrari is a company that has a passion to it, and at the same time has a unique marketing sensibility to how they promote it and how they take care of their audience."

They are also two companies that have stayed relevant for a long period of time in businesses that can be cyclical. Lauren says,

The car that started Ralph Lauren's love affair with Ferraris was a 365 GTS/4 Daytona Spider (left). After seeing one in London, Lauren was intrigued to find out more about the cars from Maranello.

Lauren's Ferrari 250 GTO, with the serial number 3987, had a great deal of racing success in the hands of another well-known U.S. entrepreneur, Roger Penske, back in the days when he was best known for his race driving.

The designer, who considers cars to be moving art, adds that the Testa Rossa, ". . .has great details, even in the way the shift knob is shaped. Every detail on the car is an art piece as far as I'm concerned."

✤ *"I love the sensibility of the Testa Rossa* in that it has all the racing elements and yet is very usable. I have a pontoon-fender TR that is totally drivable anywhere I want to take it."— *Ralph Lauren*

"Quality and passion are very important. You can't just say I have this company, but I love to do other things. You've got be totally involved with it all the time. The excitement of what my next idea is going to be, the next move, the next look, is a part of me and is with me whether I'm on vacation or working or traveling.

"If you're a fan of cars you want to see what's next, what's the new power, the new handling, technology, and shape. I think Ferrari more than most cars has that excitement because of its rhythm. A Ferrari is elegantly flamboyant, which is exciting to me. They have the passion and you can feel it.

"I'm a big Porsche fan too, but they have more restraint in their sensibility. More of a tighter sensibility. The car drives the way the car company is. Both are great, but they are very different.

"The key is how to move forward and at the same time not give up the heritage, which is who you are. There are other cars out there shooting at you, trying to get your market, adding more horsepower, getting a new sound, whatever is happening. You have to be on top of it and at the same time not give up the integrity of what you stand for." **F**

❖ *"Every detail on the car is an art piece*
as far as I'm concerned."— Ralph Lauren

GRAND TOURING AND SPORTS RACING CARS
A parting shot

WHEN PORSCHE ANNOUNCED IT WOULD BUILD 25 OF ITS SPECTACULAR 917S FOR international racing for 1970, Ferrari came right back and—thanks in part to its alliance with Fiat—said it would build a new race car, the 512 S, in similar numbers to fight the German threat.

Drawing from its experience with its Can-Am cars and the 312 P, Ferrari engineered the sleek mid-engine racer with a 5.0-liter, 550-horsepower V-12. Things looked promising after an early victory at Sebring. Although the 512 S proved it could chase the 917s, it couldn't catch them, and Sebring was its last major victory.

Ferrari reworked the car for 1971 as the 512 M, but now it was a machine for privateers like Roger Penske to race. Again, there were many high-place finishes at major events, but

no wins. Maranello had turned its attention to a smaller sports racing race car, the 312 PB. This was essentially a full-bodied version of the team's Formula 1 car, powered by a 3.0-liter flat-12. In 1971 it was no match for the Porsches or, for that matter, the Alfa Romeos designed by former Ferrari man Carlo Chiti.

Come 1972 and Porsche's withdrawal, the 312 PBs were dominant, winning every race of consequence except the 24 Hours of Le Mans, which Ferrari did no enter.

After this stunning success, Ferrari backed off in 1973, did little to further develop the 312 PB, and was overtaken by the French Matra firm. There were two wins—Italy at Monza (Ferrari's home ground) and the tricky Nürburgring—but that was it.

In fact, that it was it for 21 years. Ferrari backed out of racing sports cars. It did get behind the development of a proper race version of the Berlinetta Boxer, which resulted in some top-10 finishes at Le Mans and the venerable competition Daytonas thundered on, but Scuderia Ferrari, as the team was known, was off doing other things. F

Ferrari based its 312 PB sports racing car, with its flat-12 engine tuned to 450 horsepower, on its Formula 1 machine. These cars dominated every place they ran in 1972— except Le Mans where they weren't entered—and easily won the Constructors' World Championship. The team of drivers was impressive: Mario Andretti, Jacky Ickx, Helmut Marko, Arturo Merzario, Sandro Munari, Carlos Pace, Ronnie Peterson, Brian Redman, Clay Regazzoni, and Tim Schenken.

• Sam Posey and the 512 M

Artist
Sharon, Connecticut

Sam Posey, author, painter, architect, and one of the more articulate men to have driven race cars.

IT ISN'T ENOUGH THAT SAM POSEY IS ONE OF THE UNITED STATES' MOST EXPERIENCED RACE DRIVERS, having competed from the mid-1960s until 1981 in everything from Trans-Am pony cars to Indy cars to Formula 1. Posey is also one of the most articulate drivers. These days he spends his time writing, painting, and designing homes,

but sat down in his Sharon, Connecticut, studio long enough to describe what it was like to race Ferrari 512s for Luigi Chinetti's North American Racing Team in the famous French classic, the 24 Hours of Le Mans.

"At Le Mans in 1971 we had the 512 M, which was a pretty potent machine. Mr. Chinetti had always liked to have me start the race in the car because I would follow directions. I would drive the car slowly at first when everyone else was whizzing off. I didn't like doing that, but saw the wisdom of it, because 23 hours later many of those guys who rushed off were gone."

It's an approach that worked. Posey was in the highest placed 512 in both the years—1970 and 1971—the big mid-engine Ferraris were raced at Le Mans. In 1970, he finished fourth overall partnered by Ronnie Bucknum, one of 11 512s entered in that race. The following year he was third with Tony Adamowicz, best of the eight 512s run in 1971.

"So I started the race in 1971 and got a couple of laps in and the damn oil pressure warning light came on and the oil pressure was shaky. I figured I've got to pit. I couldn't risk blowing the engine up. I stopped and they determined it was the fault of the signaling system in the car and, in fact, there was plenty of oil pressure and not to worry about it. Disregard the light. So back out I went and the track was empty. I came out about half a lap back from the field of cars and it was a beautiful afternoon. It seemed to me that it was legit to try and catch up in order to get back a little of that lost time. I loved driving the car, so off I went."

So what was it like to drive a lap of the famous 8.4-mile Le Mans circuit?

"You'd come flying by the pits and there was no signaling," Posey begins. "That was done from the signaling pits (halfway around the circuit off the slow Mulsanne Corner in the days before reliable car-to-pit radio communications, back when signboards were used to signal the driver). That rise up into the first turn was like you were weightless and you very quickly sort of floated up to the right. The stands had big crowds on both sides and for a second you didn't really feel like you were on a road, but on some sort of amusement park ride, flowing up.

"They didn't have a chicane then (to slow the cars) and you'd come over the top of the rise and then you knew you were on a road because you were fighting to turn the car and crest the hill at the same time. It wasn't a place where you'd hang it out, but it was a little tricky.

"Then you'd come down into the esses and the car settled as you turned left. The Ferraris had pretty heavy steering so you had to muscle up a little bit to get that. You'd never consciously think of this when you were out there, but there was a slight residual idea that you were at Le Mans in a Ferrari and you felt it most at the esses because the photographs from that set of corners are so famous.

"The esses were quick. First you'd hit that left apex and then the right apex and the road did a sort of funny straightening and then dropped a little bit and kicked you out to Tertre Rouge… a quick sequence… boom, boom, boom.

"Then you were on to Tertre Rouge, a right turn that was easy for me to take. The apex was a little on the downhill and a lot of drivers would get a bit sloppy there. For some reason, I'd get it right and you'd come out next to a line of trees on your left and their white-painted trunks would flash by… whoosh, whoosh, whoosh… as you started the long, high-speed Mulsanne Straight.

"This is where the Ferrari came into its own and you could really sense the difference between it and other cars. It's a cliché to say the Ferrari engine would just sing, but it did. As the V-12 climbed up the revs you'd feel an

✦ *"It was terrifing.* **A lap was just over three minutes and you'd come into a fog bank or patch and you didn't know if it was bigger or smaller than the last time."** — *Sam Posey*

affinity for the mechanical aspects of the 512. You weren't afraid it was about to fail. In many cars you'd think, 'How is this thing going? It's got to blow up any minute.' With the Ferrari you felt it was never going to blow up, that this was what it wanted to do. Like a guy who enjoys running marathons or doing pushups, it just liked this kind of work.

"Down the Mulsanne Straight it was, well, down the straight."

Posey puts that so modestly. Each lap he was hitting and holding just shy of 220 mph along the 2.3-mile straight in the Ferrari as he and Adamowicz averaged 127.4 mph for 3,045 miles during the 24 hours. If you want to get a sense of what the drive was like, buy the DVD of Steve McQueen's movie *Le Mans* and watch the final Ferrari 512 versus Porsche 917 battle. Be sure to turn the sound up very loud.

Then there was also the danger of early morning fog on the Mulsanne Straight. Posey continues: "It was terrifying. A lap was over three minutes and you'd come into a fog bank or patch and you didn't know if it was bigger

The pedal box of a Ferrari 512 S.

or smaller than the last time, because it would change. Sometimes it would be completely clear until you got to the fog, which would be sitting there like a big pillow across the track. You'd rush into it and think, if this is a little fog bank I'm out in a split second and everything's cool, but if it's big, what then? So if it went on for one split second longer than you thought it should, the terror set in because now you imagined other cars in there, some going much slower than you, cars you could rear end at high speed.

"I had some terrible experiences in the fog, which doesn't come anymore. Mention it to a contemporary Le Mans driver and he doesn't know what you're talking about. I figure it must have been coming off the fields and the woods, but they've so industrialized the area it just doesn't happen anymore."

Whoever laid down the original public highways that became the Mulsanne Straight threw the drivers a curve, actually a kink slightly uphill and to the right near the end of the straight, a high-speed trap for an unaware driver.

"From the time you'd done the downhill out of Tertre Rouge onto the Mulsanne

Straight, you were doing a countdown to the kink. You were watching the traffic around you keenly because you knew if you arrived at the kink abreast of somebody you were in trouble. So if you were going to breathe it (back out of the throttle slightly), you wanted to breathe it so you would go through right behind the guy and if a faster car was coming up on you, you had to work that out too... a mental exercise to go through. And the kink was always tough on the big cars. You had to be alert and snick it in, and there was a bit of banking.

"You'd come over the rise after the kink and down to the Mulsanne Corner. The Ferraris were never great brakers so you'd probably be on the binders a little earlier than the rest of the guys, taking your time going down through the gears and then sort of scraping around Mulsanne. It's not that great a turn and then there were the signaling pits on your right so you were either buoyed up by your lap time or you weren't or they might not be showing you your time, which was probably more often the case.

"Then began that unbelievably fast part

Sam Posey in a 1970 Ferrari 512 S at Lime Rock Park.

that no one seems to know about, just as fast as Mulsanne. You'd go tearing through the woods, little right-handers and then there's an optical effect. The right-hander with no name before the Indianapolis Corner had a little dip before it that you couldn't see. The road just went down a little bit. There was a guardrail around the outside of it and your headlights picked up the guardrail, but not this little dip, which made you think you were closer to the turn than you were. Everybody lifted off, got into the dip and then saw the road and got back on the throttle up to the turn. Every lap it took this little gesture of remembering not to do that instinctive thing, but to hold your foot down through this period when you couldn't see the road properly.

"Then the right-hander before Indianapolis was so fast you could sling it through there, though Indianapolis didn't matter because it was just a short run to Arnage so if you didn't take a full line through Indianapolis it didn't mean anything… much better to come rushing in there as it was very effective for overtaking.

"Arnage was neat, a real feeling of driving

✤ *"It's a cliché to say* **the Ferrari engine would just sing, but it did."**
— *Sam Posey*

through the country, the town in front of you, though you didn't go into it, but made a right turn toward the Porsche Curves.

"I was lucky enough to run the old course in 1966 (co-driving a Bizzarrini GT) with the White House corner and all that… whew, that would put hair on your chest.

"The Porsche Curves were just ordinary race stuff and kind of cambered in a way that was unpleasant to drive. The road suggested a higher speed than you were able to achieve. I love it when it's the other way around and you're going faster than it looks like you can. You get this terrific sense that this is really racing.

"Then you came around to the pits again. Some courses have a place where you sense a lap begins, but I never had that sense at Le Mans. It was like the start/finish line and the lap could have started on Mulsanne or at Arnage. A lap was a wonderful collection of impressions and experiences.

"If you've done a really fast lap you often are a little mentally worn out. The idea of going for a yet faster one has little appeal. You try to back up the really fast lap with a good one to show the pits you're not slacking off, but at the same time you're kind of consolidating your gains. With the 512 M, you wanted to go faster every time. It was so delightful to drive that it welcomed you into its embrace for another lap. Let's do this dance again… and then again and again. You never felt like you wanted to quit driving the car."

Eventually he had to, of course, and Posey pitted to hand the 512 over to Adamowicz and to get a brief look at the character of Luigi Chinetti, the man who trusted Posey to be conservative early in the race.

"The last lap before I pitted during my stint," Posey says with a smile, "was a lap record. It didn't hold up, but was the record for the time being. I got out of the car just as they were announcing the record. There was a smattering of applause and I saw Mr. Chinetti looking over and he was grinning. And then he saw that I could see him, turned away and wiped the grin off his face. He was still a racer (a three-time winning driver at Le Mans) and he wouldn't have admitted he liked the record lap, but he did." **F**

The 512 S owner's manuel provides the cold starting procudure as follows: "Under cold weather conditions 10°C or 50°F or below, it is necessary to pre-heat the fuel distributor with hot water, a hair dryer, or by similar means to avoid the risk of seizing of the distributor unit which could cause irreparable damage."

• Brian Redman
Race driver, vintage motorsports event organizer
Vero Beach, Florida

In 1972, Redman shared this 312 PB with Clay Regazzoni at the 24 Hours of Daytona finishing fourth over all.

MOST FERRARI FANS REMEMBER BRIAN REDMAN AS PART OF THE ALL-CONQUERING 312 PB TEAM IN 1972, which won every race in the sports racing championship that year but one—Le Mans—where they weren't entered.

That was actually Redman's second stint at Ferrari. First time around was in 1968, when Redman was a hot property. He raced for John Wyer's Ford GT40 team, John Cooper's Formula 1 team, and, "I was still driving my Formula 2 Lola T100 and had a terrific race at Crystal Palace near London where I put it on pole by some miracle against Jochen Rindt and Jacky Ickx. I finished second in the race to Rindt and about that time was asked to go to Ferrari and test the Formula 2 car, which I did.

"I tested with Mauro Forghieri and at lunchtime he said to me, 'Brian, you see over there under the trees? That is *Signore* Ferrari. . . . '

"What he meant, of course, was, 'Go faster . . . . '"

Redman laughs when he tells the story today and adds, "The only time I met Enzo Ferrari was after the test. I was invited to lunch at Maranello. There must have been 40 or 50 managers eating there and Ferrari was at the far end of the room. As I'm standing in the door he stood up and he was a very imposing figure. He came walking toward me and stopped in front of me. I started to put my hand out, but before I got the chance to do anything he stuck his right hand out and gripped the left side of my cheek between his fingers and shook vigorously. And he said the only two words he ever said to me: 'Nice boy.'"

As a result of that test day, "They asked if I would like to drive the car at the Nürburgring in a few weeks' time. This was on the south circuit, which is similar in character to the main circuit, but only about five miles around. In practice I came in about 15 laps from the end of the last session on Saturday and Forghieri was shouting and yelling, 'Why do you stop? Why do you stop?'

"I said I'd gone as fast as I can.

"He said, 'Go out and try harder, you are in tenth place.'

"So I went out and drove hard and went a tenth of a second faster… and it seems I'd been in fourth place all along.

"The race started and Ickx, who was the team leader, was leading. Second place was Piers Courage, third place was Kurt Ahrens, and I was fourth.

"On the fourth or fith lap, just after we passed the pits, there was a tremendous blow in my left eye. A stone came up and went through my goggles and it felt like it had hit me in the eye. I saw stars. I flung my hand up, threw my goggles off and came to halt. I found when I was blinking that I could see, and drove relatively slowly without goggles the rest of the lap—probably four miles—and stopped at the pits. Forghieri rushed up and said, "What's the matter? What's the matter?'

"I replied, 'It's my eye. . . .'

"He replied, 'It's okay, it's okay, wear your spare goggles.'

"I didn't have any so he told me to take Ickx's, which were dark green sun goggles.

✦ "I said, 'If I drive for Ferrari I'll be dead by the end of the year'" — *Brian Redman*

Down in the forest bits where there is no sun I couldn't see very well, but I was highly fired up and finished fourth in the race and set a new lap record.

"When I got into the hotel bedroom, I just sat on the bed and I was almost in tears. I just sat there thinking, Christ. . . .

"That night at dinner Forghieri left the table and came and said, 'I speak with *Signore* Ferrari and for the rest of the year you drive Formula 2 and at the end of the year Formula 1.'

"And I said, 'No thank you.'

"He said, 'What do you mean no thank you?'

"I said, 'If I drive for Ferrari I'll be dead by the end of the year.'" 🅵

Redman in 1972. This postcard was part of the "mondial marche '72" brochure for the 312 PB team.

Sebring 1972, below, Redman/Regazzoni failed to finish due to a fire.

Grand Prix

GRAND PRIX
Back in the groove

AFTER THE DISMAL LAST HALF OF THE 1960S, JACKY ICKX'S THREE WINS AND CLAY Regazzoni's one victory in the pretty 1970 312 B looked good. Mario Andretti won the first race of the 1971 season for Ferrari and Ickx had another, a sole victory in 1972 and nothing in 1973. But then the Lauda era began.

Luca di Montezemolo was now in charge of the team and hired young Austrian Niki Lauda to partner with Regazzoni. They had three victories in 1974 with the aging 312 B3, but then Mauro Forghieri did himself proud. The car he designed was called the 312 T, and with it Lauda won five Grands Prix and Regazzoni one in 1975, earning the World Championship for Lauda and the constructors' title for Ferrari.

Lauda almost won again in 1976 in the 312 T2. He won five of the first nine races, took second in two others and third in another. Then he suffered a terrible accident in the German Grand Prix, so badly burned and injured that he was given last rites by a priest. Remarkably, Lauda fought back, missed only two races, and continued to score points, but in the final event of the year, in Japan, he withdrew instead of racing under the dangerous wet conditions, basically handing the title to James Hunt.

Lauda proved his worth in 1977 when he came back, won three races, and finished second six times, giving he and Ferrari the championships again.

Previous pages: Gilles Villeneuve won the pole, set fastest lap, and won the 1979 Long Beach Grand Prix in a Ferrari 312 T4. This was one of six Grands Prix won by Maranello as it handily took the constructors' crown. Villeneuve's teammate, Jody Scheckter, won the World Championship that year. Jacky Ickx finished second in the 1971 Spanish Grand Prix (below) in a Ferrari 312 B.

For 1978, Lauda went to the Brabham team and Carlos Reutemann and Gilles Villeneuve were Maranello's driver line-up. Reutemann won four Grands Prix, while Villeneuve took his home race, the Canadian GP. Sometime Ferrari driver Mario Andretti won the driver's title in a Lotus-Ford, becoming only the second U.S. citizen to do so.

South African Jody Scheckter replaced Reutemann for 1979 and won three races among his 11 top-5 finishes to take the World Driver's Championship, Ferrari again winning the constructors' title. ◨

Here you can see how Ferrari Grand Prix cars changed in the 1970s, from the early 312 Bs (left) to the 312 B3 and T series of the mid-decade and the Niki Lauda/Luca di Montezemolo years when Maranello dominated.

In 1976, Road & Track *had the chance to road test a Ferrari 312 B3, thanks to Harley Cluxton. The magazine enlisted the help of Formula 1 champion Phil Hill to put the car through the test, which yielded a 0-60 mph time of 2.4 seconds, 0-100 mph in 4.3 seconds, with the quarter-mile in 9.0 seconds at a speed of 159 mph. This was with gearing that put the top speed at an estimated 192 mph. The Ferrari had a test weight of 1655 pounds and was propelled by a 3.0-liter flat-12 developing 490 horsepower. Hill said, "Little by little I found the Ferrari had marvelous control and was extremely honest as far as integrity in a machine is concerned. Handling and control were just fabulous."*

*Austrian Niki Lauda on his way to winning
the 1975 Monaco Grand Prix in a Ferrari
312 T. Lauda and Ferrari won the driver's
championship and constructors' titles that
year, and then repeated the same thing in
1977 with the 312 T2.*

Gilles Villeneuve, the great Canadian driver, won six Formula 1 races for Ferrari and finished second in the 1979 World Championship. He was killed practicing for the 1982 Belgian Grand Prix. Mauro Forghieri, the famous Ferrari engineer, says, "Villeneuve was a force of nature, a natural who did the maximum in every moment, a man who gave everything for the show. This is the reason the public loved him, doing the maximum at every moment, even when the car was not very good."

*Gilles Villeneuve in
a Ferrari 312 T3.*

Andretti winning the 1971 Questor Grand Prix at Ontario Motor Speedway in the 312 B.

• Mario Andretti

World Driving Champion, 1967, retired
Nazareth, Pennsylvania

IF THINGS HADN'T WORKED OUT, MARIO ANDRETTI COULD HAVE GROWN UP IN MARSHAL TITO'S Communist Yugoslavia. The U.S. would have been denied a living legend, a man who has won the Formula 1 World Driver's Championship, the Indianapolis 500, the Pikes Peak Hillclimb, the Daytona 500, the Sebring 12 Hours, several USAC championships, and countless midget and sprint car races.

When Andretti's hometown of Montona, Italy, was about to be partitioned off as a piece of post-war Yugoslavia, the family moved to a refugee camp in Italy. There, twin brothers Mario and Aldo were drawn to racing. Mario explains: "Ferrari was it. If motor racing caught your imagination as an Italian kid, it was because of Ferrari. Trailing very close were Maserati and Alfa Romeo. Those were my formative years, up to the mid-1950s when I was in Italy.

"Ferrari was really more of the magic side. It remained that way for me, and it captured the imagination of the rest of the world that is interested in motor racing.

"You talk about Ferrari and I don't care where you are, what corner of the planet you are in, people will know what you're talking about."

Mario and Aldo would get to watch segments of events like the Mille Miglia or Giro di Toscana, and then, "Two gentlemen—Sergio and Bepe—who knew we were going to the States (the Andrettis emigrated in 1955) told us, 'Before you leave, we want to take you to the Italian Grand Prix in Monza.' That was quite the treat, to see my idol, Alberto Ascari. He didn't win, but I almost got more out of it by watching him wrestle that Ferrari against the Mercedes of (Juan Manuel) Fangio.

"So Ferrari was magical for me and I always kept that in mind. Once I started racing I figured that some day I'm going to get a taste of that."

How ingrained was the thought of racing a Ferrari? It's 1963, Andretti's racing career is taking off, not on road racing circuits like Monza in sleek Ferraris or Maseratis, but on tough little bullring ovals in the eastern U.S. driving upright midget race cars.

Andretti laughs and remembers, "I'm sitting in a midget, having the day of my life, about to win the third feature race of the day, which was never done. Three feature races, Labor Day

1963, one in Flemington, New Jersey, two in Hatfield, Pennsylvania. And I'm sitting in the cockpit, just about to get started in that last race of the day in an Offenhauser midget and I don't know why, but do you know who the heck came to mind?

"Dan Gurney, who had driven for Ferrari, and I'm thinking, 'I wonder what Dan Gurney would be doing if he was sitting here?'"

It would be three more years before Andretti got his first chance to drive a Ferrari, but then, "I drove for Chinetti in 1966 with Pedro Rodriguez (they were fourth in the Daytona 24 Hours in a 365 P2/3) and I felt at home in a Ferrari right away. Then I was called to do the Monza 1000 kilometers. One thing led to another and I developed a relationship with the old man.

"I was part of the Ford team in 1966 and 1967—the Le Mans program and all that—and then I think it was in 1970 when Ferrari was testing at Daytona with Arturo Merzario, who had no idea what to do with the banking. He was running low, downshifting going into the banks.

"I got a call from Mauro Forghieri (then Ferrari team manager) and he asked if I would go down and help them with the test. Of course I went. I think the first lap I was 11 seconds quicker. I had done 24-hour tests for Ford when we were barreling into the banking at 220 mph with the Mark IIs and Mark IVs. There was no chicane at the time, so once you got on the banking you did the whole thing and I was flat all the way around."

Andretti's first drive in a Ferrari Formula 1 car, the 1971 South African Grand Prix, resulted in the driver's initial F1 win. Soon after, he drove a Ferrari to win both heats of the Questor Grand Prix, an odd event that mixed F1 and Formula 5000 race cars at the now-defunct Ontario Motor Speedway, east of Los Angeles.

"After I won in South Africa and then both heats of the Questor Grand Prix, Ferrari said, 'You have to drive for us,' and that year at the Nürburgring, where I finished fourth he was even more impressed. He really wanted to hire me but it just didn't work out with the contracts I had."

But they kept trying.

"In 1977, even before I won the Italian Grand Prix (in a Lotus 78-Ford), Mr. Ferrari

✦ **"After I won in South Africa** *and then both heats of the Questor Grand Prix, Ferrari said, 'You have to drive for us.'"* — *Mario Andretti*

wanted to hire me. He said that at the end of the year he wanted to talk and we had it planned that after the Italian Grand Prix I would go to Maranello.

"Meanwhile, I already had a handshake with Colin (Colin Chapman, owner of the Lotus team) for the following two years. The reason I didn't do a long-term with Colin even then," Andretti chuckles, "was because of finances. Colin was like that… difficult.

"So I won at Monza, which put me even more in a position of strength and Colin didn't want me to go to Maranello. I told Colin I had a meeting with Mr. Ferrari. He said, 'Mario, we have a handshake, don't go, it's going to complicate matters.'

"I said, 'Colin, I have to go and I have to see what my opportunities are.'

"I always did things my own way.

"So I went and we sat there, my wife and I, in front of Ferrari in the office. We talked about everything and then it came down to something that's not very pleasant over there, because the culture is different when you talk about money. I said, 'Well, what are you willing to pay me?'

"And he said, honest to God, 'I cannot put a price on your talent.'"

Andretti laughs, explaining, "He threw it right back at me. I was thinking, actually I

Mario Andretti and Mauro Forghieri at the 1971 Monaco Grand Prix. Says Andretti: "I love Mauro and his energy. He was brilliant, but typically Italian—a lot of confusion. I loved to drive for the guy. . . he brought a lot to Ferrari."

shouldn't be doing this. It's best if I just throw him a number he won't be able to meet and that will be the end of the story. So I threw him twice what my new contract for Lotus was going to be. He didn't hesitate for one second and said, 'Okay.'"

A shocked Andretti explained to Enzo Ferrari, "Now, to be honest with you I was expecting you not to accept that and he said, 'Well, if that's your price, that's your price.'

"So I said, 'Now what do I do?'"

Ferrari answered "Well, that's what we have lawyers for."

Andretti replied, "Look, I'll leave and let's sort of let it lie for a day or so."

So they shook hands.

"The next day," Andretti continues, "I get a fairly long Telex from Ferrari. Meanwhile, Colin Chapman had called him and to this day I don't know exactly what was said, what went on, but Ferrari wrote in the Telex that he had lawyers and was ready to deal on those terms, but after having the long conversation with Colin Chapman, 'I think you should remain with him.'

"I said, 'Not so fast, give me another day.'
And he said, 'Take all the time you need.'

"So I called Colin and I said, 'Colin, fine,
you're trying to determine my future. I have a
tendency to want to stay with you because
of what I think we can accomplish, what we
have done, and where we can go in the
future. My main motivating factor has never
been the financial side, but I've always gone
for the best contract because that's how I
justify my racing ultimately for my future, my
family, and all that. Once my financial side is
stable, then I'm very serene and very happy.

"He said, 'I can't meet that.'"
Andretti replied, "Well, then you don't
want an unhappy driver on your team. I'll give
you until tomorrow."
The following day Chapman called and
doubled Andretti's contract.
"I would have gone either way. Obviously
it's better I stayed because I came away with
a championship, but nevertheless I think I
could have won a championship for Ferrari
sooner or later because they weren't the
fastest car, but they had the reliability, and we
didn't have that at Lotus." **F**

*Mario Andretti started the 1971 season
by winning the South African Grand Prix
in a Ferrari 312 B2. Seen here he is
trying to qualify for the Monaco Grand
Prix, though his Indy 500 commitments
meant his only attempt was on a wet
track, making it impossible to get onto
the starting grid.*

• Brenda Vernor

Living legend
Maranello, Italy

HER GIVEN NAME IS BRENDA VERNOR, BUT TO MANY WHO HAVE VISITED FERRARI OVER THE YEARS SHE IS known simply as, "La Brenda."

Raised in England, Brenda had made several trips to Italy when she was asked to teach English in Modena and ended up working as a secretary for another native of Great Britain, Ferrari driver Mike Parkes.

Growing up in England Brenda thought racers were "a bunch of silly buggers running around the same track all the time," and had no interest in them. Through her work with Parkes, Brenda began to meet racing people and follow the sport. It turned out to be a different world with an atmosphere she never imagined, one that quickly drew her in.

Eventually, she became Enzo Ferrari's secretary and explains that, "For the Old Man, every day started the same. He'd go to Modena in the morning to the barber for a shave, then to the cemetery to visit the grave of his son and, later, his wife. Then to his office in Modena—which is now a parking garage—until about 10:30. He'd be here in Maranello in his office in the racing department by 11:00. Mr. Ferrari would stay until lunchtime—1:00 or 1:15—when he'd go to Fiorano to eat and stay until about 4:00. Then back into the office until 7:30 or 8:00. And he did this even when he was 90."

Brenda obviously enjoyed working for Enzo Ferrari, and not just because he was a big fan of her chocolate cake. "He was a wonderful man. Good fun. He'd get angry and shout, but after 10 minutes it was all finished. And he'd never insult anyone. He used to like to tease people and play jokes. And he was very discreet. Everyone respected him. Even when he was 90 years old, people at the factory would whisper, 'The Old Man just came in. . . . ' And he'd say 'good morning' to everyone."

In the racing department, Brenda found a world populated by 199 men and no other women, a situation she seems to have relished. She particularly enjoyed working with the drivers. She recalls those first years in Modena and her contact with those drivers, like the days when Parkes, Lorenzo Bandini, and Ludovico Scarfiotti, "did the durability tests for the road cars. There was no autostrada then, so they drove from Modena to Napoli and back nonstop. And I had the

three of them—Mike, Lorenzo, Lulu—at home. One would be driving, one sleeping, and I'd be cooking for the other. Lulu and Bandini liked to have fun. They'd play tricks on me, like locking me in the bedroom or the bathroom and I couldn't get out… those were very enjoyable times.

"Lorenzo Bandini lived in the same block of flats I did, and every morning he'd come by, we'd have breakfast, and he'd take me to school in his car. He was a lovely guy, and he was good fun. Lorenzo was like a brother, a great friend."

"I was at Monte Carlo when Lorenzo had the accident," Brenda adds, remembering Bandini's fatal crash in 1967. "I said I would never go again, and didn't go for more than 10 years."

What was it like around the Ferrari factory when a driver died? "No comment from anyone. Work just continued. The Old Man wouldn't show his feelings. What could you do? It doesn't change anything. But you have those feelings inside, even if you don't show them. It was the same when Gilles was killed."

Remembering the great Gilles Villeneuve, Brenda recalls, "Many of these drivers called me their 'mother'." She smiles and adds, "'Aunt' would have been better." But then you understand how she rightfully earned the title when she tells about Villeneuve having to be in Modena for testing during August even though most establishments were closed during that traditional vacation month.

He was bored and asked, "Haven't you got a spare bed in your apartment?" Brenda didn't, but she slept on the sofa and gave the driver her bed. "Gilles only ate *tortellini alla panna* and a filet steak with chips (french fries)," she remembers. "Can you imagine in the middle of August, as hot as it was, me cooking in the kitchen, making *tortellini alla panna* and steak with chips for Gilles?" And she tells it like a mother (or an aunt) who might sound like she's complaining, but obviously wouldn't have it any other way.

Brenda calls the Canadian driver an introvert. "But if you knew him, he was a nice guy." And then she gets defensive about the drivers. "You know, many people judge drivers without really knowing them. I always defend them. No one is perfect and they have their defects, but they are often misunderstood.

"That's why I always defend Rene Arnoux," she continues. "His appearance was misleading, with long hair, sometimes a bit greasy, but he's the most human person I've ever met. To look at him you might not think so, but I remember how he once organized a dinner for 50 handicapped children in wheelchairs. He organized the bus and the restaurant, he gave them presents, and you should have seen him with those children. He has a heart of gold, and if he can do a favor for you, he'll do it."

Brenda continues talking about Ferrari's drivers in no particular order:

Carlos Reutemann: "I shall never forget. I was sitting in Dott. (Franco) Gozzi's office typing something. There was a knock on the door. I said 'Come in' and in walked a handsome man, tall, blond, suntanned… and I just stood there with my mouth wide open. Carlos is so relaxed and laid back."

Chris Amon: "A great friend who was very unfortunate. It seemed that every race he drove he was in front, but something that cost 100 lira would break and poor old Chris would be left there. He was such a good test driver, one of the best we ever had… and such a nice guy.

"Chris never learned Italian. I had to do everything for him. He'd get me to read the newspapers for him on Monday after a race. You know how hard Italian journalists can be on Ferrari drivers. I'd never read Chris the truth, because he'd get so upset, or I'd tell him I didn't have time to read the newspaper to him. I felt so badly for him because he didn't deserve it."

The late Michele Alboreto: "A nice guy, very generous. If you needed anything or you needed a favor, he'd do it. I often went to Milan for a weekend with Michele, his wife and their kids. And I never saw him angry."

Patrick Tambay: "A gentleman. He was the only one I cried for when he left."

Gerhard Berger: "I love him. First of all, in my opinion he's one of the most handsome guys in the Formula 1 business. And a wonderful character. People often say Austrians are cold, but that's not true."

❖ **"Chris Amon:** *A great friend who was very unfortunate. It seemed that every race he drove he was in front, but something that cost 100 lira would break and poor old Chris would be left there."* — Brenda Vernor

Jean Alesi: "He's a very nice boy, always smiling. He has those beautiful blue eyes… and he will always say 'Hello,' regardless of where you see him or who he is with."

Didier Pironi: "Another man who was great fun. They'd be testing at the circuit and the Old Man would be there, and Didier would reach back and undo my bra in front of the Old Man, who used to laugh his head off at that."

Jody Scheckter: "Funniest guy in the world. Lots of people didn't understand him. They call him 'the bear.' But if you go to dinner with Jody you will be under the table with laughter, with his dry humor."

Clay Regazzoni, the Swiss driver who was left a paraplegic after a racing accident in the 1980 Long Beach Grand Prix, and who was recently killed in a road accident: "He's one to admire. When you knew how Clay was, a bit of a playboy, and what happened to him… yet he was always laughing, always had a joke to tell. He was the toughest, and I admired him very much."

Ask about the funny side of the drivers and she immediately brings up: "Jody, Gilles, and Didier," and begins talking about the great drivers as though they were pranksters.

Brenda tells about a quick ride to a lunch with Villeneuve in the mountains above Maranello that involved trying to keep her tortellini down on the way back to the factory.

Or the time Villeneuve and Pironi were supposed to be testing at Fiorano at 8:30 in the morning, but couldn't be found anywhere. "I called the Fini Hotel, but they said that while I'd booked the pair, they never arrived.

"Panic set in because everyone was at the track, waiting for them. I remembered they had been with a guy from Milan and I got his phone number and called. He said, 'Yes they're in a hotel here in Milan.' I phoned them and said, 'What the hell are you doing there? You're suppose to be testing this morning.' They said, 'Alright, we're leaving now.' They got into Gilles' 328 and made it to Modena in 40 minutes. When they got to the autostrada exit at Modena Nord, there were policemen with machine guns because the two had passed every toll barrier without stopping. When they got to the barrier here and the police found out who they were, all they asked for were autographs. And Gilles and Didier arrived at Fiorano at half-past nine." 🄵

Patrick Tambay

Rene Arnoux

Michele Alboreto

Jody Scheckter

Didier Pironi

Jean Alesi

The 1980s

The 1980s

PRODUCTION CARS
The generation of the 288 GTO and F 40

FERRARI MADE ITS FIRST PRODUCTION CAR CHANGE OF THE NEW DECADE IN March 1980 at the Geneva Motor Show. The Bertone 308 GT/4 was replaced by Pininfarina's Mondial, another handsome (if not beautiful) small 2+2 with a mid-mounted 3.0-liter V-8. Three years later it was joined by a soft-top cabriolet version, a true 4-seat Ferrari convertible. In 1985, both cars got 3.2-liter V-8s, which grew to 3.4 liters in 1989 when the pair was also fitted with a transverse gearbox.

In 1980 Pininfarina teased us with the Pinin, a 4-door Ferrari show car, a beautiful shot up a dead-end street.

The Berlinetta Boxer was finally replaced with another big, mid-engine exotic, the Testarossa. Even now, decades later, there's controversy over the car's Pininfarina styling,

In 1980, Pininfarina teased us with this 4-door Ferrari sedan concept.

particularly the side strakes leading back to rear radiators. It retained the flat-12 of the Boxer, now at 390 horsepower.

In 1984 we saw the first of a new type a Ferrari, a safety- and emissions-certified street machine with a true race car edge. Looking like a 308 that had been to the gym, the 288 GTO was quite a different machine. Originally meant for Group B competition, the GTO has a 2855-cc V-8 mounted longitudinally, fed by a pair of IHI turbos that bump output to 400 horsepower. The 288 GTO was never raced and only 272 were made, so it remains a rare and valued Ferrari.

Several of us were at Ferrari's test track when we saw a 288 GTO with even more muscle. Turns out this was a prototype for the 1987 F 40, a car built to celebrate the company's 40th anniversary. Based on Formula 1 technology, and made of Kevlar and carbon fiber with a shape fine tuned in the wind tunnel, the F 40 has a 2936-cc twin turbo V-8 with 478 horsepower.

Race driver and F 40 owner Dario Franchitti tells us, "It must be a soul thing. I'm not blind to the fact that not every Ferrari is perfect, but when I get in my F 40 I really appreciate it. If you are in a bad mood, you get out of the Ferrari feeling great." Ferrari ended the 1980s with the long-awaited replacement for the 308/328. Called the 348 for its 3.4-liter V-8 engine, it has 300 horsepower and a longitudinal powerplant, like the 288 GTO. **F**

By 1985, Ferrari was ready to upgrade its best-selling sports car. With the addition of a 3.2-liter, 270-horsepower V-8 the 308 became the 328. This 328 is parked in front of the entrance to the Fiorano test track.

During the 1980s, Ferrari had a 4-seat convertible, the Mondial Cabriolet. Launched in 1983, Ferrari refined the Mondial, available in both convertible and hardtop versions, throughout the decade. Initially powered by a 3.0-liter 240-horsepower V-8, the car received a 3.2-liter, 270-horsepower V-8 in 1985, and a 3.4-liter, 300-horsepower engine in 1989.

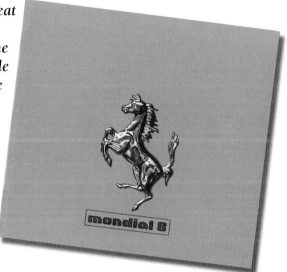

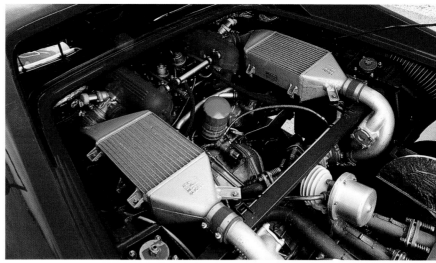

Ferrari resurrected the GTO name in 1984 on a limited-series model originally meant for Group B racing. Looking like a muscular 308, the wide-fender 288 GTO has a twin-turbo, intercooled 2.8-liter V-8 with 400 horsepower V-8 (above). Unlike the V-8 in the 308, it is mounted longitudinally. Ferrari kept the car's weight down with advanced materials such as carbon fiber. When Group B ended, the 288 GTOs became highly prized road cars. At the left, a 288 GTO sits next to its well-known namesake, the 1962 250 GTO.

The Testarossa replaced the Berlinetta Boxer in 1984. It retained the 5.0-liter flat-12, now rated at 390 horsepower and was certified for sale in the U.S. Pininfarina's exterior design of the "TR" was dramatic, to say the least, but had it critics, then and now. If you think the rear view at the right looks wide, you should feel how wide the car seems from the driver's seat.

Above: Ferrari presented the final iteration of the 412, now with a 5.0-liter, 340-horsepower V-12, at the 1985 Geneva Auto Show. Left: After the long production run of the 308/328, Ferrari followed up with the 348 TB. While the Pininfarina shape was an evolution of the earlier series, the 348s had a new internal structure and the 3.4-liter, 300-horsepower V-8 was now placed longitudinally in the chassis.

• Dario Franchitti and the F 40

Racing driver
Nashville, Tennessee

Born in Scotland, Dario Franchitti has had a distinguished racing career, mainly in CART and IRL cars, but he also harbors a love of Ferraris.

DARIO FRANCHITTI IS ONE OF THOSE RARE SUCCESSFUL MODERN RACE CAR DRIVERS WITH AN appreciation for race cars from the past. He is an annual participant in the Goodwood Revival, the most famous (and arguably hairiest) vintage car races in Europe.

On many weekends during the race season his ride is the number 27 Dallara-Honda, which he drives for the Andretti Green team in the Indianapolis Racing League; on other weekends he and his brother, Marino, co-drive the Andretti Green team's Courage-Acura sports racing car in the American Le Mans series. On an off weekend he might be flying his Eurocopter AS350 B3 helicopter.

Given his druthers, however, there's a good chance Franchitti would be home in Scotland, rushing down a two-laner through the moors in his Ferrari F 40, the 4-wheel manifestation of his lifelong love of the cars from Maranello.

"It started with my dad," Franchitti explains. "I was born in 1973 and when I was really young he had a blue Ferrari

Dino 246 GT. Between that and watching Grand Prix races with him, seeing the Formula 1 cars with Niki Lauda, Gilles Villeneuve, Jody Scheckter, Clay Regazzoni, all those guys, it really started there.

"He transferred that passion down to me and I've always loved Ferraris. There's a mystique about them, the badge... it's difficult to explain.

"I've had five Ferraris. My first was a big mistake, a 348, but I was 21 and put it down to that. Then I had a Testarossa, which was okay. Handled like a shopping cart, but really went pretty well in a straight line. Then I got my 355 Spider, which was my first new one and I still own that car. I love it and really enjoy driving it whenever I get a chance.

"Then I got serious and bought an F 40. If I ever had to sell everything, the F 40 would be the last thing to go."

He then acquired an F 430 Spider but it didn't suit his tastes and Franchitti sold it about four months later.

The driver of the latest in modern race cars explains his love of the 20-year-old F 40: "As a kid I had a poster of one on my wall so I always wanted an F 40. When I was coming up in Formula 3, I went to a track day at Knockhill in Scotland and a guy asked if I wanted to drive his F 40. I couldn't believe that a car was so fast and handled like a race car. . . the sensations it gave. After a number of years when I began to earn good money in Champ Car, I started to look for an F 40 and when I managed to find one that was one owner and low mileage I bought it.

"On the roads we have in Scotland, which I think are the best in the world, you can have so much fun with the F 40, starting with the explosive acceleration. Compared to a modern car, does it handle that well? Not really, but you have to work for every mile an hour you carry through a corner and I love that. It is massively fast and so raw, no sound-proofing, none of that stuff, the closest to a race car I've ever driven on the road.

"I keep both Ferraris in Scotland because I can get more road use out of them, though my schedule makes that difficult. I only put about 70 miles on the F 40 last year, but they were great miles.

"One of my teammates, Tony Kanaan, has a Porsche Carrera GT and when I start getting excited about a 1961 Ferrari 250 GT short wheelbase and such, generally my teammates look at me like I'm slightly mad.

"The problem with modern supercars is that to explore their limits on the road is

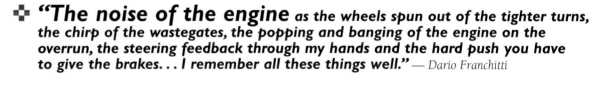

✦ **"The noise of the engine** *as the wheels spun out of the tighter turns, the chirp of the wastegates, the popping and banging of the engine on the overrun, the steering feedback through my hands and the hard push you have to give the brakes. . . I remember all these things well."* — *Dario Franchitti*

impossible. In the F 430 you had to be doing a crazy speed down a country road to get excitement out of it. You get in the F 40 and you're going a bit slower through a corner, but having an absolute blast.

"Modern supercars are great for showing how much engineering progress has been made, but I like to enjoy a car at the limit and older cars allow me to do that."

Franchitti offers an example: "About four years ago my cousin and I were going to visit some friends in the west of Scotland about and hour and a half drive from my house. We loaded the car (as much as you can) with our stuff and headed off. After about half an hour of motorway driving we were on the sort of roads you see on TV used for tarmac stages in the World Rally Championship. Pushing the F 40 pretty hard on these roads over the moors of Scotland for an hour was almost as tiring as driving the Indy car. The suspension travel is pretty limited so the car spent most of the time with all four wheels off the ground!

"The noise of the engine as the wheels spun out of the tighter turns, the chirp of the wastegates, the popping and banging of the engine on the overrun, the steering feedback through my hands and the hard push you have to give the brakes. . . I remember all these things well.

"The concentration required to keep the car on the limit made it all the more rewarding. It was a drive that really sticks in my memory as one of those times when, in my mind, I was driving a lap of the Targa Florio," Franchetti says, referring to Sicily's famous race run on a 45-mile open-road circuit but discontinued as an international event after 1973 for safety reasons.

I once asked Franchitti if the dangers inherent in racing decades ago would have kept him from racing if he'd been born in that era?

He didn't pause a second before saying, "Absolutely not."

A true racer's racer. **F**

• Sam Posey & John Morton on Luigi Chinetti

SAM POSEY CALLS LUIGI CHINETTI "AN IRON MAN." POSEY, WHO DROVE FOR CHINETTI, ELABORATES: "HE HAD endurance. Look at his whole life; he just hung in there with a limited set of ideas in his head for how things would go, but so devoted to those ideas that he could make mountains move where people seemingly brighter and more with it could not.

"He was the most un-with it guy at the time, up against the modern race car people, wearing his coat, tie, and little Legion of Honor pin.

"To Mr. Chinetti, a car was a Ferrari. There was no other car. If they weren't Ferraris they were just contraptions. And Ferraris came from the factory and that's the way they were. You didn't fuss with them. You didn't adjust sway bars or tune the engine. You'd change gears, but everything else was a given.

"In the early 1970s that was no longer the case in racing. Everything was adjustable and you were obliged to adjust things like crazy to get the car set up properly. He knew what was going on, but just wouldn't participate in it."

And Chinetti's way worked.

Roger Penske's race team, which is renowned for its ability to take any race car and make it better, bought a Ferrari 512 M to race in 1971.

Posey explains: "Here's Mr. Chinetti just taking the car as it comes from the factory, not touching it, not doing anything, and our cars are running great. And here's Penske with all his tweaks and knowledge and they could never get the damn thing going as fast as they should have." (Chinetti 512 Ms finished ahead of Penske's three of the four times they competed against each other.)

John Morton, one of the United States' most versatile road racers for decades, drove for Chinetti on numerous occasions. In recalling his drives in Chinetti's Ferrari Boxers in 1981 and 1982, Morton explains that Chinetti, "was an incredible guy because he stayed up most of the night in that suit, standing there watching the car. It was such an honor to drive for him, because early in my awareness of racing he was almost the factory team for Ferrari. He had a lot of good old stories about the Mexican road race, things like that. (Chinetti co-drove to a win in that difficult event in 1952 with Piero Taruffi, driving a Ferrari 212.)

"Chinetti's team felt like an anachronism, like actually going back in time. After night practice we'd go have a nice dinner at the hotel. They prepared it especially for him and it was really good.

"They didn't have to ask, 'Are we having fun now?' because they were having fun. And you knew it. I almost felt like a spectator to what was happening and thinking, 'This is neat, because this is how it was.'"

At Le Mans you're basically up all Saturday night, the race finishes at 4 p.m. Sunday, and then you're celebrating or commiserating.

❖ "To Mr. Chinetti, a car was a Ferrari.
There was no other car. If they weren't Ferraris they were just contraptions." — *Sam Posey*

Chances are, you'll be up late again.

Morton remembers Monday morning this way: "People would start wandering down, the mechanics, the crew people, and Chinetti, and pretty soon we're all around this big breakfast table. I'd already eaten cereal because I thought that's what you do, but now we're having a big breakfast and the topic at the end of the meal is where we're going to eat lunch. Most of the conversation wasn't in English, so I asked where it was and it was 20 miles down the road, so right after breakfast we got in our cars and drove to a huge fancy lunch.

"Today, they'd already be on planes headed back to the shop to download data." **F**

Luigi Chinetti— complete with sportcoat, tie, and Legion of Honor pin—in the pits at Le Mans in 1982 with the NART Ferrari 512 BBLM that finished ninth overall.

Above, a NART-entered Ferrari 365 GTB/4 Daytona at Le Mans in 1973, one of its co-drivers being Luigi Chinetti's son, Luigi Jr.

Grand Prix

GRAND PRIX
Highs and lows

LIFE WAS AT LOW EBB ON THE FERRARI GRAND PRIX TEAM AGAIN AS THE DECADE began. The 1980 season saw the switch from the normally aspirated 312 T5 to the turbocharged 126 C. The team scored no wins in 1980. Typical of the year in 1981, Gilles Villeneuve managed to win two races—Monaco and Spain—but retired from 8 of the year's 15 Grands Prix.

Then 1982 hit the ultimate highs and lows, the latter being the death of the popular Villeneuve while practicing for the Belgian GP at Zolder. His teammate, Didier Pironi, suffered severe leg injuries at the German GP, ending his good shot at the World Championship. In the end, however, Ferrari accumulated enough points to win the

Previous pages: After winning the World Driver's Championship in 1979, Jody Scheckter wore the coveted number 1 on his 1980 Ferrari 312 T5 Grand Prix car.

constructors' title. Thanks to the efforts of drivers Michele Alboreto and René Arnoux, the Scuderia took the constructors' title again in 1983.

Alboreto won three more races over the next two seasons and garnered enough points in 1985 to finish second in the driver's standings. But the team came up dry in 1986, although Austrian Gerhard Berger won the final two races in 1987 and had a wonderfully sentimental race in 1988, taking the Italian GP at Monza less than a month after Enzo Ferrari died.

Formula 1 returned to non-turbo engines for 1989—a V-12 in Ferrari's case—and John Barnard's F1/89 design, with which Englishman Nigel Mansell won two races and Berger won one event. A feature of the car, later adapted to Ferrari road cars and now almost standard on high-performance automobiles: a semi-automatic gearbox actuated by levers on the steering wheel. **F**

In the early 1980s, Formula 1 cars had explosively powerful turbocharged engines. Ferrari won the constructors' title in 1982 and 1983 with its turbo cars and finished second in 1984 with the 126 C4 seen here. The 1.5-liter wide-angle V-6 (above) had a pair of KKK turbos and a claimed 660 horsepower at 11,000 rpm in race trim. For qualifying, the V-6 was pumped up to more than 800 horsepower.

Below: Enzo Ferrari had an ambitious goal: win the Monaco Grand Prix, the 24 Hours of Le Mans, and the Indianapolis 500. To compete at the famed Brickyard, Ferrari built a car in 1986 that conformed to the U.S. CART series specifications. The open-wheeler used a 2.6-liter, 690-horsepower turbocharged V-8, but Maranello never raced the car.

• Mauro Forghieri on Gilles Villeneuve

Race engineer
Modena, Italy

NO ONE EVER DOUBTED THE BRILLIANCE OF ENGINEER MAURO FORGHIERI'S DESIGNS DURING HIS
several decades with Ferrari. There are seven constructors' titles and four World Driver Championships to prove it.
Mario Andretti says, "I love Mauro and his energy. He was brilliant, but typical Italian… a lot of confusion." Andretti

tells about a pit stop at Sebring in 1970 when the Ferrari 512 S he was co-driving won, but
needed fuel just before the finish. "I had to come in 1 or 2 laps from the end because I never
would have made it… the reserve light came on. Of course we had no radios and all that, but
they were ready for me anyway. I had to turn the engine off and jump out of the car while it
was being refueled and Mauro was there to pick me up and threw me right back in. Never
buckled up and off I went. I think I killed about 14 photographers on the way out.

"I loved to drive for the guy, and he was brilliant. He brought a lot to Ferrari."

And no one ever doubted the native driving talent of Canadian Gilles Villeneuve—winner of
six Grands Prix for Ferrari, second in the driver's championship in 1979—nor his determination
and enthusiasm… perhaps too much enthusiasm at times.

One of the most spectacular drivers in Grand Prix history, Villeneuve was killed during
practice for the 1982 Belgian GP. Villeneuve was what Forghieri calls "a force of nature, a
natural who did the maximum in every moment. If you compare him to Niki Lauda, Lauda is a
man who is using his brain continuously, but not giving too much to the public.

"Gilles was a man who gave everything for the show. This is the reason the public loved him,
doing the maximum at every moment, even when the car was not very good."

In 1981, when Formula 1 cars could use normally aspirated or turbocharged engines, Ferrari
was backing its 580-horsepower turbo V-6. Forghieri proudly recalls: "We did a beautiful win at
Monte Carlo and in Spain. We showed the turbo engine could be a winner in Monte Carlo.
Nobody believed it before."

Those proved to be the only wins for Ferrari and Villeneuve that season. The team was
having problems with fuel and pistons, Forghieri explains, so for the Dutch Grand Prix, "we had
a new engine with modifications almost ready when I left for the race." Forghieri asked that

✦ ***"Gilles was a man who gave everything*** *for the show. This is the reason the public loved him, doing the maximum at every moment, even when the car was not very good."* — Mauro Forghieri

the engine be sent when it was ready and they would test in Zandvoort. "It would have been nice to know the result from the dyno and from the track, which is the most important part."

The engine arrived on Saturday afternoon, late, and they put it in Villeneuve's car. Before the race start, Forghieri asked, "Please, Gilles, you have the experimental engine in your car. It's very important for us to do the entire race and compare it with the other, but also to have 300 kilometers under racing conditions to see if the pistons are okay or if we have the same problem."

Villeneuve said he knew what he had to do. Forghieri went back to the pits for the start. The flag dropped and almost immediately Villeneuve started passing cars. He launched over the back of Bruno Giacomelli's Alfa Romeo and ended up airborne and then into the fences.

Forghieri can now smile about it: "He came walking back and he didn't have the

courage to come close to me.

"But he was a tremendous driver, fully honest and completely in love with racing." ⅃

Gilles Villeneuve finished third in the 1982 Long Beach Grand Prix in a Ferrari 126 C2, only to be disqualified because of the unique two-piece staggered rear wing that the Tyrrell team claimed was illegal.

The 1990s

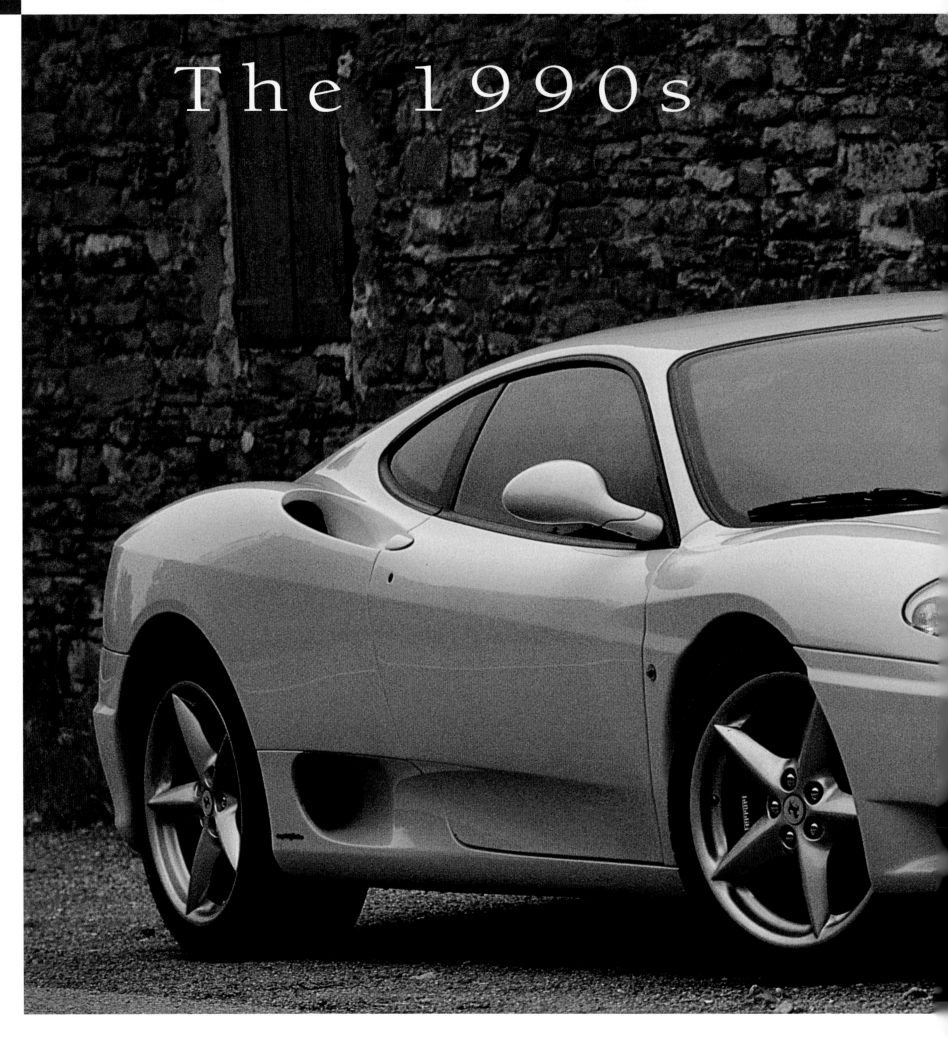

Previous pages: Ferrari upped the ante in the exotic car world in 1999 when it started production of the 360 Modena. While aluminum had long been used for the engines and bodywork of supercars, Ferrari designed the 360 to also have an aluminum chassis. Pininfarina designed the body and did extensive wind tunnel work to create a total aero package for the 360, from its visible shape to the unseen undertray. The 3.6-liter 40-valve V-8 produces 395 horse-power, which is enough to get the Ferrari to 60 mph in 4.3 seconds. Price? Just shy of $150,000.

The 1990s

PRODUCTION CARS
The Montezemolo era

THE 1990S BEGAN WITH A BIT OF UNCERTAINTY AT FERRARI, WHICH HAD BEEN stumbling a bit in the years since Enzo Ferrari's death. Luca di Montezemolo returned to the company in 1991 to begin the renaissance, but with the long turnaround times in the

automobile business it would a few years before the results showed.

The Testarossa went through two changes to the 512 TR and the 512 M, lifting horse-power to 428, then 440. The elegant 456 GT 2+2 with a 5.4-liter, 442-horsepower V-12 was added in 1992, while a Spider version of the 348 was launched the next year.

We really didn't see the "Montezemolo" cars until the F 355 Berlinetta and GTS in 1994, followed a year later by the Spider version. From the first time we drove the F 355, those of us who had been testing Ferraris for years knew this was different… a thoroughly modern car with electronic suspension adjustment, a 3.5-liter, 380-horsepower V-8 and a transverse 6-speed gear-box. Come 1997, it would get the first civilian version of the F1 semi-automatic transmission.

A worthy successor to the F 40, the F 50 was offered to celebrate Ferrari reaching the half-century mark. Like the F 40 it is a raucous street machine that reflects Formula 1 technology. . . and features 520 horsepower from its V-12.

Those of us who were never enamored of the Testarossa's mid-engine, big-behind footprint were delighted when its successor, the 550 Maranello, had its V-12 mounted up front. And we were thankful for the suspension's electronic stability control system.

In the last year of the century, Ferrari replaced the F 355 with an even more modern model, the 360 Modena. Working with Alcoa, engineers created an entirely aluminum car: chassis, body, and engine. This 3.6-liter 400-horsepower V-8 was offered with a 6-speed transmission or the latest F1 electrohydraulic paddle shifters. ▣

In the 1990s, Ferrari upgraded the Testarossa, keeping the displacement at 5.0 liters but increasing the horsepower to 428 in 1992 and then to 440 two years later in the 512 M.

When Ferrari replaced the popular
365/400/412 2+2 it did so with an equally
well-done model: the 456 GT. The leather-
upholstered interior and the ride are quite
comfortable and yet the car is no slouch on
a twisty road. The 5.5-liter V-12 produces
442 horsepower and generous torque for
easy driving and a 0-60 time just over
5 seconds.

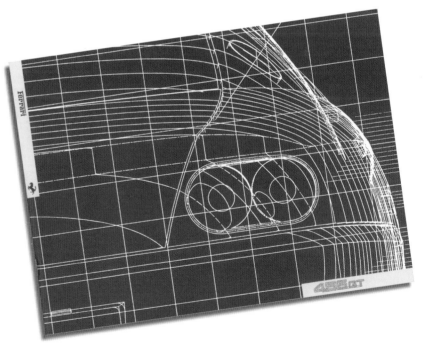

Appropriately, Ferrari first presented its 348 Spider to the public in Beverly Hills in 1993 and the folding-top 2-seater went on to be one of those models everyone seems to enjoy. Introduced with the 348's 300-horsepower V-8, the rating was subsequently upped to 320 horsepower, resulting in a 0-60 mph time of around 5.5 seconds. Here the 348 Spider is seen with the factory-built replica of its first car, the 1947 125 S.

At right: The heart of two generations of
Ferrari exotic cars: the big aluminum
flat-12 engine. Below: Beginning as a
4.4 liter with 380 horsepower and
24 valves in the 365 GT/4 Berlinetta Boxer,
it grew to 5.0 liters, 440 horsepower,
48 valves, and full compliance with
emissions laws in the 512 M.

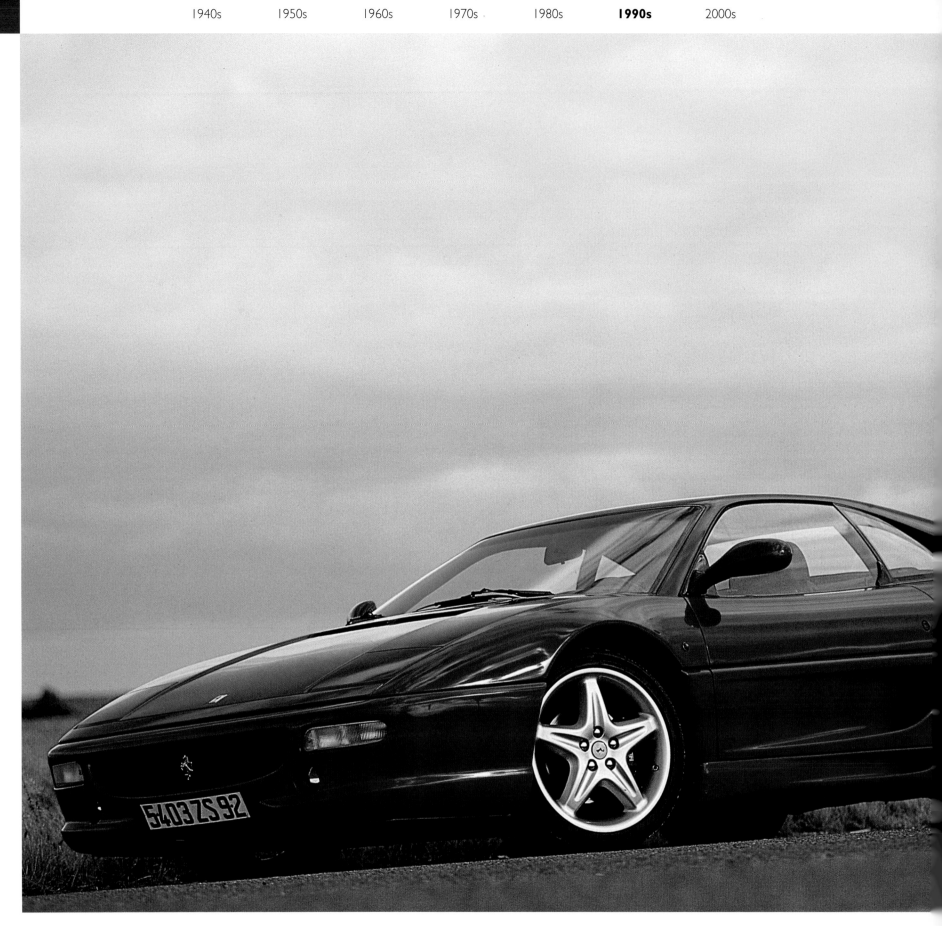

*First of the Montezemolo-era Ferraris was the
F 355 from 1994, which was done as a Berlinetta
coupe or GTS targa. With a 3.8-liter 380-horse-
power V-8 and a suspension that can be firmed
at the flip of a switch, the F 355 proved to be a
nicely balanced machine at speed.*

Above: An F 355 Challenge car, part of the successful series that Ferrari established for its owners and has continued through the 360 Modena and F 430.

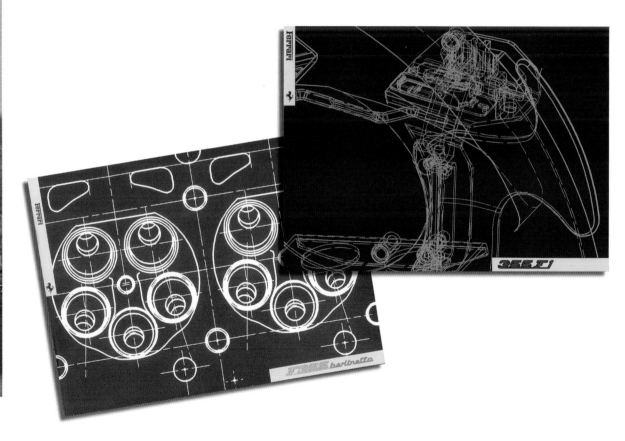

For 1995, Ferrari began building the F 355 as a Spider, the first convertible from Maranello with a power folding top. Here it is being driven by Road & Track's Editor-In-Chief, Thos L. Bryant. Race driver Dario Franchitti's first new Ferrari was an F 355 Spider. "I love it, and really enjoy driving it whenever I get the chance."

To mark its 50th anniversary, Ferrari created the F 50. With a targa top that allowed for an open or closed cockpit, the car is based on a central carbon fiber tub with Formula 1-derived suspension. Weighing just 2249 pounds, the F 50 is powered by a normally aspirated 60-valve 4.7-liter V-12 that is also based on F1 technology. Pininfarina did the design work, and Ferrari built 349 F 50s between 1995 and 1997.

Ferrari's model line-up in the mid-1990s in the courtyard of the Fiorano test track. From the left: the 456 GT 2+2, 550 Maranello, F 355 Spider, and F 50.

Many of us were delighted when Ferrari launched the 550 Maranello. For one thing, the press introduction was at the Nürburgring in Germany, where we were given rides by Michael Schumacher or Max Papis. Better yet, Ferrari had abandoned the mid-engine, wide-backside layout of the Testarossa for a traditional front V-12 design. And Pininfarina redeemed itself after the TR with the svelte, athletic styling of the 550 Maranello. The car above was photographed on the Futa Pass, which was part of Italy's famous Mille Miglia road race.

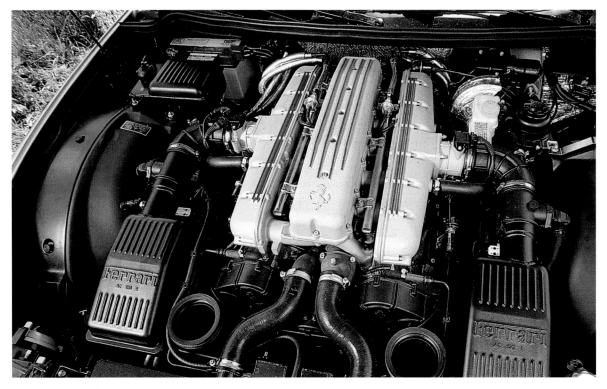

Ferrari equipped the 550 Maranello with a 5.5-liter V-12 (left) that produced 485 horsepower. Mated to a 6-speed manual gearbox, the V-12 will propel this grand tourer to 60 mph in 4.7 seconds on its way to a top speed a few ticks short of 200 mph. The interior (right) is upholstered in leather and is luxurious. Ferrari built the 550 Maranello from 1996 until 2003 when it updated the design with minor exterior changes, took the engine out to 5.7 liters and 540 horsepower and called the car the 575 M. This was the first time Ferrari offered a V-12 with the semi-automatic F1 transmission.

SPORTS RACING CARS
Back for a limited engagement

FERRARI MADE AN OFFICIAL RETURN TO SPORT RACING CARS WITH THE 333 SP. Powered by a 650-horsepower 4.0-liter V-12, the open-top prototype was created for U.S. IMSA competition, where it was the championship-winning car in 1995. In a career that stretched to 1999, the 333 SP won both the 12 Hours of Sebring and 24 Hours of Daytona, and was raced quite successfully in Europe. **F**

Ferrari's last attempt at a factory sports racing car came in the late 1990s with the 333 SP. Above it is seen in the courtyard at the Fiorano test track with the factory-built replica of Ferrari's first sports racer, the 125 S. Right: a 333 SP decelerates for the hairpin in the 12 Hours of Sebring.

Two three-time winners of the 24 Hours of Le Mans: Phil Hill and Luigi Chinetti. The latter was responsible for putting young American drivers in racing Ferraris.

• Phil Hill's Obituary for Luigi Chinetti

Ferrari Importer
Greenwich, Conn.

WHEN LUIGI CHINETTI DIED IN 1994, *ROAD & TRACK* ASKED ITS LONGTIME CONTRIBUTOR, 1961 FORMULA 1 World Champion Phil Hill, to write an obituary. One of many drivers Chinetti helped throughout the years, Hill, who won the championship in a Ferrari, wrote:

It would be difficult to imagine Ferrari being successful in America without the efforts of Luigi Chinetti. Even though the cars from Maranello seemed destined to become legends in the U.S., Chinetti, who died recently at age 93, was the principal force in the whole process.

In the beginning, funds for supporting Ferrari's racing programs were in short supply. Chinetti dealt with this by selling Ferraris in the wealthy American market. He was a master at placing the cars in the hands of the best customers… and making certain they paid top dollar.

Chinetti was all too aware of the importance of Enzo Ferrari's race cars being driven by the right men. In some cases that meant selling them to talented and influential amateur drivers, like the late Jim Kimberly. Other times he sold the cars to men who could afford to put promising drivers in Ferraris, men like Allen Guiberson and George Tilp, who sponsored beginners like Richie Ginther, Dan Gurney, and myself.

The North American Racing Team (NART) was formed by Chinetti to enter Ferraris in American races and at Le Mans. In 1964,

✤ *Luigi's fame selling Ferraris overshadows his driving career and yet, like me, he was a three-time victor at the 24 Hours of Le Mans, winning in 1932 and 1934 in Alfa Romeos and in 1949 with a Ferrari 166, when he drove all but 20 minutes of the race.* — Phil Hill

Enzo Ferrari was battling with the Italian automobile club, and his Grand Prix cars were entered in the U.S. Grand Prix by NART, painted white with a blue stripe. The following year, a NART-entered 250 LM scored an upset win at Le Mans with Masten Gregory and Jochen Rindt driving. Other NART drivers included Mario Andretti, Ricardo and Pedro Rodriguez, Bob Grossman, and Sam Posey.

Milan-born Chinetti's relationship with Enzo Ferrari began in the 1930s, when he worked and raced for Alfa Romeo and Ferrari managed the team. Moving to France in the late 1930s, Chinetti then traveled to the U.S. as part of the Lucy O'Reilly Schell Maserati Specials team that had Rene Dreyfus as one of its drivers for the Indianapolis 500. Stranded in America by World War II, Chinetti stayed, meeting his future wife, Marion, with whom he had one son, Luigi Jr.

Visiting Europe after the war, Chinetti met with Ferrari and soon began importing his cars into America. The first was a 166 Spider Corsa sold to Briggs Cunningham. Hundreds more followed.

Luigi's fame selling Ferraris overshadows his driving career and yet, like me, he was a three-time victor at the 24 Hours of Le Mans, winning in 1932 and 1934 in Alfa Romeos and in 1949 with a Ferrari 166, when he drove all but 20 minutes of the race. Chinetti co-drove a Ferrari with Piero Taruffi to win the 1951 Carrera Panamericana. I was paired with him in his last race as a driver, the 953 12-hours at Reims.

Chinetti had a special talent for both getting himself into very good cars and aligning himself with people able to support him, then making the best of it.

Chinetti's forte was his cleverness in managing the power he derived as Enzo Ferrari's agent. He was, however, both praised and scorned for this, depending on one's particular involvement.

Over the years, Luigi became endeared to practically all who had known him, especially those who he had helped in their formative racing years. He derived great pleasure and satisfaction in helping so many of us young drivers get started. In the end, all of us felt deeply indebted to him. ꓣ

Grand Prix

GRAND PRIX RACING
Moving up the ladder

WITH THE STRONG TEAM OF ALAIN PROST AND NIGEL MANSELL, FERRARI WON 6 of the 16 Formula 1 races in 1990 before being completely shut out the following year, when Prost's and Jean Alesi's seasons were riddled with retirements. In fact, Ferrari wouldn't win a Grand Prix again until July 1994 when Gerhard Berger was the victor in the German GP. Jean Alesi won once again the following year.

But Montezemolo was on the case, hiring Frenchman Jean Todt to head the F1 effort. For 1996 he tempted World Driving Champion Michael Schumacher from the Benetton team. With Schumacher came technical wiz Ross Brawn and chassis designer Rory Byrne. This brain- and talent-trust got busy, resulting in Schumacher winning three times in 1996, five in 1997, six in 1998, and two in 1999 before breaking his leg at the British Grand Prix, after which teammate Eddie Irvine took a trio of wins.

Scuderia Ferrari was primed for the new century. ⓕ

Left: Irishman Eddie Irvine, Michael Schumacher's teammate in the latter part of the 1990s, driving the Scuderia's V-10-powered F 300, finishing third in the 1998 Monaco Grand Prix. Above: Jean Todt (left) and Michael Schumacher celebrate after another Grand Prix win. This happened increasingly as the team gathered strength in the late 1990s, with Schumacher winning nine Formula 1 races in 2000.

Luca di Montezemolo, far right, observes the management of the Formula 1 team at Monaco in 1973 before assumming control. Georgio Ferrari (no relation) standing on the pit wall was team manager. Jacky Ickx' wife appears uninterested.

• Luca Cordero di Montezemolo
Chairman, Ferrari S.p.A.
Maranello, Italy

LUCA CORDERO DI MONTEZEMOLO IS ONE OF THOSE INDUSTRY TITANS WHO SEEM TO HAVE A magic touch.

Born in Bologna, Italy in 1947 to a Piemontese family that has produced leaders for centuries, Montezemolo is a lawyer by education, including studies at Columbia University in New York. His ties to Ferrari go back more than three decades, and he is currently chairman of Fiat and chairman and president of Ferrari.

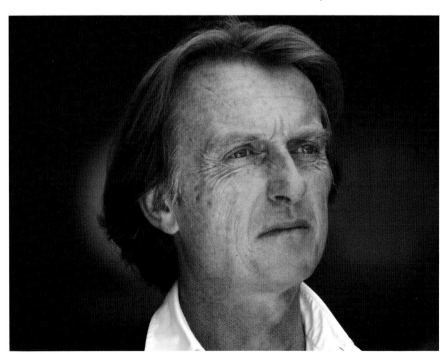

Mobbed like a rock star at motor shows, Montezemolo still makes time to talk about his passion for Ferrari at length with us. We asked what names he considers important to Ferrari during his years with the company.

He begins by pointing out that of the current management team, "I am the oldest of the group because I started with Ferrari in July 1973. I am still there as the chairman in 2007, so it's a long story.

"If I was to give you some names. . . .

"Number one is, of course, Enzo Ferrari. I was with him on long summer days at the Fiorano track when Maranello was deserted for holidays, working together, thinking of the future, taking decisions, looking ahead. . . long days in August. Ferrari was a difficult man, but with a fantastic vision.

"Niki Lauda. In 1974 I chose Niki, supported by Enzo Ferrari, after (Ferrari Formula 1 driver) Clay Regazzoni was the first to give me a good report about him. He joined the team in 1974 as a young, rather unknown Austrian driver. He became champion of the world twice, 1975 and 1977, and he was for sure in a position to win in 1976 without the crash (a near fatal accident during that year's German Grand Prix)."

Montezemolo mentions engineer "Mauro Forghieri, a very creative, intelligent, and difficult character. He was crucial in that period of the company (1960s and 1970s) in terms of capability. I remember the Ferrari 312T of 1975 was superb."

He continues with more Ferrari Grand Prix drivers, saying in his clipped Italian accent, "Carlos Reutemann, an Argentine gentleman, a good-looking man and a very, very nice person. Unbelievably quick in qualifying, not fantastic in the race, but a big support for Ferrari after Clay Regazzoni's departure (after 1976).

"Gilles Villeneuve, something unique in the history of Formula 1 and Ferrari.

"Nigel Mansell was a driver in 1989 and 1990 who did fantastic races for us. He was fast and important for Ferrari, as he was able to win many races.

"I also remember Mario Andretti and Alain Prost. . . big champions for Ferrari."

Going back a bit in Ferrari's history he adds, "I cannot forget Phil Hill, the first American who was champion for us and one of the reasons we became so famous in the United States."

In late 1991, Montezemolo was named president and CEO of Ferrari to bring the automaker out of the malaise into which it had slipped after the death of Enzo Ferrari in 1988. From the period since that time he adds five names.

Three are people:

"Michael Schumacher, Amedeo Felisa (Ferrari's General Manager and chief engineer of the Montezemolo-era cars), and Jean Todt, who was extremely important to Ferrari (as the architect behind Ferrari recent long stretch of success in Formula 1)."

Two are Ferrari automobiles:

"The 360 Modena, an unbelievable car, and the Enzo, the quickest Ferrari ever made and the one I dedicated to Enzo Ferrari."

Montezemolo explains about seven-time World Driving Champion Schumacher, "Michael has been unique because first of all in the history of Ferrari no one has been with us 11 years without problems, without polemics, even in the difficult moments. And no one was able to win so many world championship titles with Ferrari like Michael.

"He was unique in terms of capability, in terms of speed, and in terms of team mentality, working very closely with the team. And in

terms of attention to detail and the improvement of the car."

And then Montezemolo goes back to the automobiles, "In the last 15 years I cannot forget our cars. Ferrari has engineered and built very innovative cars, very high technology cars. We were the first to introduce the Formula 1 gearbox, total aluminum cars. . . not just the chassis, but gearbox and engine. . . and the first to introduce an underbody very related to Formula 1 aerodynamics. And at the end of the day we have been the first to introduce the Enzo, which is more or less a Formula 1 car with a body.

"These are my memories," he finishes, but being the ever-optimistic, forward-looking executive he adds that, "the best Ferrari will be the next one." ▪

✦ **"I cannot forget Phil Hill, the first American who was champion for us and one of the reasons we became so famous in the United States."** — *Luca di Montezemolo*

Michael Schumacher on his way to winning the 1999 San Marino Grand Prix at the Imola circuit, not far from Modena, in the Ferrari F 399.

The 2000s

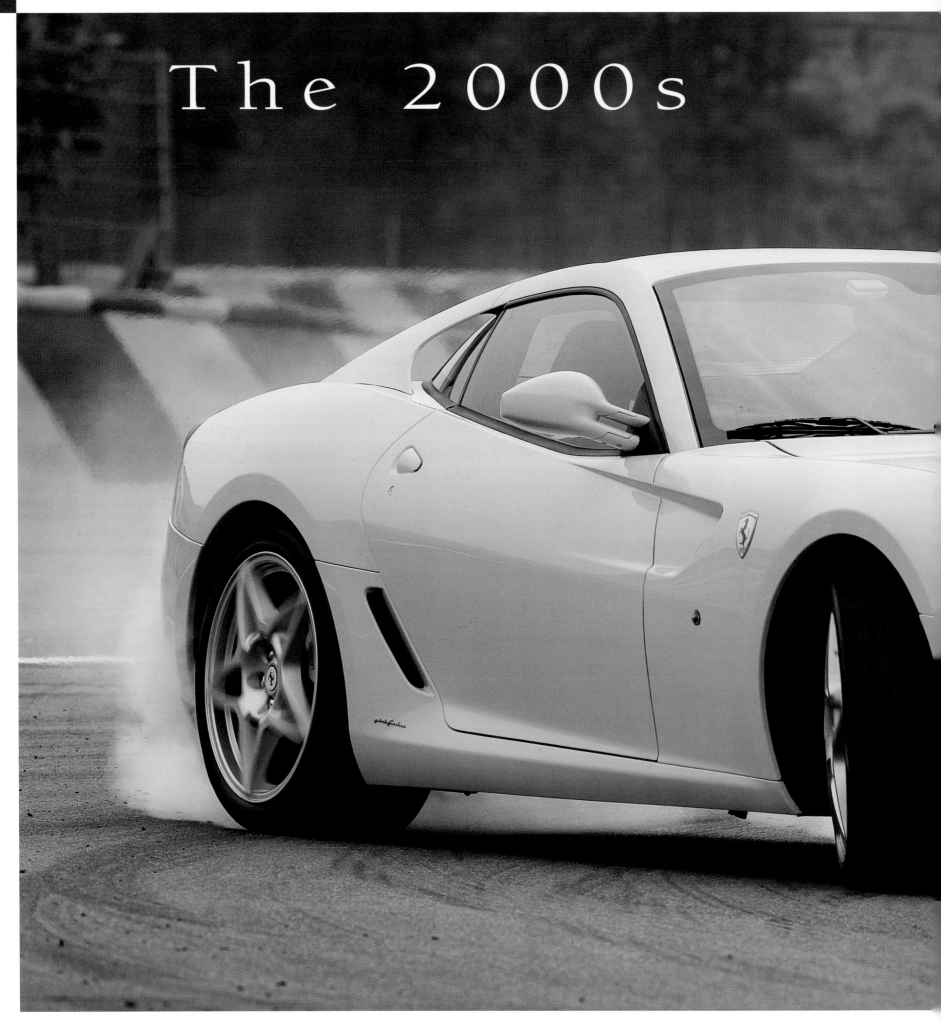

The 2000s

Previous pages: Ferrari's 599 GTB Fiorano is the successor of the 575 M. As with all new Ferraris, the body and space-frame chassis are of aluminum. Inside, of course, is an ergonomically superb driver's interior upholstered in fine leather. With a 6.0-liter, 611-horsepower V-12, the two-seater flies to 60 mph in 3.2 seconds on its way a top speed above 200 miles per hour. Price? Around $300,000.

PRODUCTION CARS
Thoroughly modern machines

FERRARI DID A CONVERTIBLE VERSION OF THE 550 CALLED THE BARCHETTA IN 2001, then updated the 550 Maranello to the 575 M in 2002, kicking the horsepower up to 540. For the first time the paddle-shifted semi-automatic gearbox was available behind a V-12.

Three years on, they created 559 examples of a version called the Superamerica with a very trick glass roof that would rotate back to lie on the trunk lid. The very clever design came from Leonardo Fioravanti, the same man who penned the Ferrari Daytona.

Then came the Enzo. Ferrari calls it a Formula 1 car with a body, a love-it-or-hate-it shape that is undeniably exciting. Fitted with a 650-horsepower V-12, the carbon-tub Enzo hits 60 mph in 3.3 seconds, aided by a 6-speed no-lift paddle shifter. Ferrari built 399 Enzos… and then one more for the Pope.

Ferrari produced the 360 Spider in 2001, and then in 2004 replaced the 360 line-up with the F 430 Coupe and Spider. Also an all-aluminum machine, the car's styling mirrors the "sharknose" front of Phil Hill's 1961 F1- and Le Mans-winning cars. An evolution of the 360, the F 430 has a 4.3-liter V-8 and is one of the most delightfully power-flexible sports cars in the world. Several well-prepared competition F430s are proving to be a match for racing versions of the Porsche 911.

Also in 2004, Ferrari replaced the aging 456 GT with the 612 Scaglietti, a proper 2+2 with surprisingly good rear seat room plus a 540-horsepower V-12 up front. Like the 360 Modena and F 430, the 612 is an all-aluminum design. Pininfarina's design of the 612 is not universally admired.

If you've driven an Enzo it's difficult to image a super-Enzo, but that is the FXX. For around $2 million, an owner buys one of the 32 800-horsepower supercars and uses it for track events.

To replace the 575 M, Ferrari shortened the aluminum chassis of the 612 to create the 599 GTB Fiorano for 2007. With a 620-horsepower V-12, paddle-shift gearbox and shock absorbers with—now get this—magnetorheological fluid, it is a technical tour de force. The wind tunnel-developed shape is contentious to some, but once you've seen one at speed, it's beautiful.

Makes you wonder, what's next? **F**

Ferrari's facilities have been turned into quite the showplace. Left: The Renzo Piano-designed wind tunnel. Below: A Jean-Yves Lechevallier Formula 1 sculpture. Bottom: The Formula 1 garage at Fiorano.

Above: The high-tech engine machining facility, which is in an environmentally friendly building.

Ferrari bodies are dipped in a cleaning solution (left) before being painted by robots in a computer-controlled sequence (above).

Top: The main Ferrari Store is located across from the factory in Maranello. There are also stores in cities such as Los Angeles, Beijing, Shanghai, and Rome. Right: Roger Penske and Steve Wynn combined to create a Ferrari dealership in the Wynn Las Vegas resort and casino. It's likely the only car dealership in the world that charges admission.

Established in 1993, the Ferrari Challenge offers the opportunity for owners to race against each other in a national series and then international runoffs in Italy.

The Challenge series now uses a modified version of the F 430 called the F 430 Challenge. It retains the looks and 490-horsepower V-8 of the standard F 430, but with numerous alterations. Among the modifications are gear ratio changes, special Pirelli slick tires, the stability and traction controls disabled, and the car's "race" mode engaged. The F 430 Challenge cars are lighter than the road versions and the suspension is developed for racing.

To celebrate several things, from Pininfarina's 70th anniversary to the 50 years of its cooperation with Ferrari to a pair of Formula 1 constructor's championships, Maranello created the 2001 550 Barchetta Pininfarina. Like a true Barchetta, it is meant for open-air driving. The windscreen was lowered 4.0 inches and a pair of rollover hoops and headrests were placed behind the driver and passenger. The drivetrain is stock 550 Maranello, with 485 horsepower from the 5.5-liter V-12.

A Ferrari 575 M Maranello leaving the traditional gate at the factory. Pininfarina made minor exterior changes to Ferrari's front-engine exotic car, but what matters most was under that long hood. The V-12's displacement was increased to 5.7 liters, with horse-power up to 515 and torque to 434 foot-pounds on a broader curve. The 6-speed transmission, which is mounted as a rear transaxle, was reworked to take the electronically controlled hydraulic F1 paddle shift system. The factory claimed a 0-60 time of 4.1 seconds and put the top speed around 200 mph.

• Richard Losee and the Enzo

Business man
Provo, Utah

THERE ARE TWO WELL-KNOWN STORIES ABOUT MEN CRASHING AND DESTROYING FERRARI ENZOS AT speed. One is about a good guy.

Good guy
Richard Losee.

The other story involves the well-publicized wreck in which one-time Swedish electronic game magnate, Bo Stefan Ericksson, managed to split his red $1.2 million Enzo in half at a reported 162 mph on Pacific Coast Highway in stylish

Malibu, California. This was an all-too-public event that ultimately brought down around him a house of cards that sent him to a state slammer for three years for embezzlement and drunken driving, followed by deportation.

In marked contrast, Richard Losee is a pillar of the community, his happening to be Provo, Utah. Businessman, church leader, and nationally recognized drug rehab clinic owner, Losee and his father are longtime car collectors. When I first met the Losees, his dad owned the James Bond Aston Martin DB5 used in the movie, *Goldfinger*, plus the Rolls-Royce driven in the same flick by Auric Goldfinger's right-hand man, Odd Job.

Ferraris have been at the heart of their collecting for decades, which is why Losee was near the top of the short list of customers who would get the mid-engine, carbon fiber-chassis Enzo in the U.S. in 2003. Since Losee is a *Road & Track* friend and reader, when the magazine heard he was getting an Enzo, it called and asked it if could test the car. Losee agreed, providing we'd come to Utah and help him drive it to R&T's offices in Newport Beach, California, to put some break-in miles on the Ferrari.

He didn't have to ask twice. Ferrari World Driving Champion Phil Hill, Road Test Editor Patrick Hong, Design Director Richard Baron, and I went to Provo and were more than happy to help. We photographed the car on the Bonneville Salt Flats and then meandered to California via back roads and few freeways, Losee giving all of us a shot at driving the car.

Here's what amazed us: The stunning, 650-horsepower, paddle-shifter, Formula 1-inspired supercar proved to be delightfully easy to drive, the only problem being keeping things reasonably legal. In Hill's hands the Enzo was a road-going race car, and once on the track in California it reset many of *Road & Track*'s road test records. How about 0–60 mph in

3.3 seconds, 1.01g on the skid pad, braking from 60 mph to a stop in 109 feet, and a top speed estimated at 218 mph?

Losee wasn't intimidated by the Enzo's horsepower or star power. In fact, Richard and *Road & Track* agreed to make the Enzo an unofficial part of the magazine's long-term, high-mileage fleet, and Losee proceeded to use it more than many men use their weekend cars. By mid-2006, he had put a remarkable 31,183 miles on the supercar, using it for everything from winning Ferrari rallies to Make-A-Wish drives to around-town driving.

And then came August 2, 2006… Losee takes up the narrative:

"Through Sean Harris, who owns the local Ferrari dealership, I heard about an event

❖ ***"We had been told there were a few undulations or*** *'whoop-dee-doos,' early on the course. However, it was reported to me by someone who had driven the road at 100 mph that it was no big deal."* — Richard Losee

called Utah Fast Pass, which is in the spirit of the Copperstate 1000, the Colorado Grand, the California Mille, and other open-road events for great automobiles.

"I thought this would be an opportunity to do something with my dad. It wasn't a serious rally, more of a three-day tour, and it was to benefit a few charities, especially the Fallen Heroes Foundation of the Utah Highway Patrol, to help the families of officers who had either been seriously injured or died in the line of duty. As we went to some of the smaller towns in Utah, Fast Pass gave money

At 650 horsepower and 485 pound feet of torque, the Enzo' 6.0-liter 48-valve V-12 will rocket the 3230-pound Ferrari to 60 mph in a mere 3.3 seconds and then on to a top speed of 218 mph.

✦ ***"When they gave me the ticket*** *they said they would have 'gone to court' that I was doing at least 206 miles per hour just prior to the accident..."*
— *Richard Losee*

for local student scholarships or to help the town improve a park or whatever they needed. It was a wonderful event.

"They made available a 14-mile closed course on a public road between St. George and Delta, Utah, on a state road. The Highway Patrol cordoned it off and the idea was that you could drive it at any speed you wanted, depending on the abilities of you and your car. The Highway Patrol would radar you and give you a ticket for the speed you attained. That ticket wouldn't go on your record, but you'd write a check for the 'fine' to the Fast Pass charity.

"We had a wonderful experience over the three days. Sometimes my dad would ride with me, and I let the commissioner and one of the captains of the state Highway Patrol drive the Enzo for a short time. They are great guys.

"The third day we were to run the special speed section. I wanted to go early because you never know what might happen and the temperature would be lower so the car would have a bit more power. If I was going to get a ticket I wanted it to be a big one.

"There were a dozen or so of us in the first group and I was the third or fourth to leave.

"The mistake I made was not taking a reconnaissance run. I'm a past SCCA (Sports Car Club of America) National Group 2 Pro Rally Champion (in 1997 in a Volkswagen Golf GTi) and though we weren't allowed in the SCCA to do reconnaissance runs, it made sense that if I was going to drive this road at very high speed I should check it out first. I had worked out an agreement with one of the highway patrolman to drive the 14 miles ahead of time, but it never happened. We never hooked up the next morning.

"We had been told there were a few undulations or 'whoop-dee-doos,' early on the course. However, it was reported to me by someone who had driven the road at 100 mph that it was no big deal. Based on that I wasn't too concerned in the Enzo with its downforce and general capabilities.

"From that point on, other than duct taping a few places on the car and double-checking things, I was just waiting to go. We'd been stationary for probably an hour while they prepped the route and I remember being ushered onto the road, but after that I have very little recollection.

"I was wearing a current full-face racing helmet. I do recall looking down at the digital speedometer once or twice and thinking that I need to keep my speed up. The next thing I remember is being in a very, very large slide off to the left-hand side of the road and thinking, 'Thank goodness my father and I had agreed that he would not go with me.' And in the middle of the slide, I recall thinking, 'This is not good.'

"The next thing I remember is about five seconds of recollections in the Life Flight, realizing I was in a helicopter. I remember being in the hospital. People say I was lucid and spoke."

Turns out Losee had, among other injuries, fractured his C1 and C2 vertabrae, suffered a concussion, and had a broken sternum, broken ribs and a broken thumb. When the Highway Patrol got to him, he had no pulse and the strap of his helmet had cut off his breathing. Luckily the first man there, Utah Highway Patrol Lieutenant Robert Anderson, knew what he was doing. He loosened the neckstrap and got Losee breathing again. Remarkably enough, Losee spent just 10 days in the hospital.

The incident made the front page of the

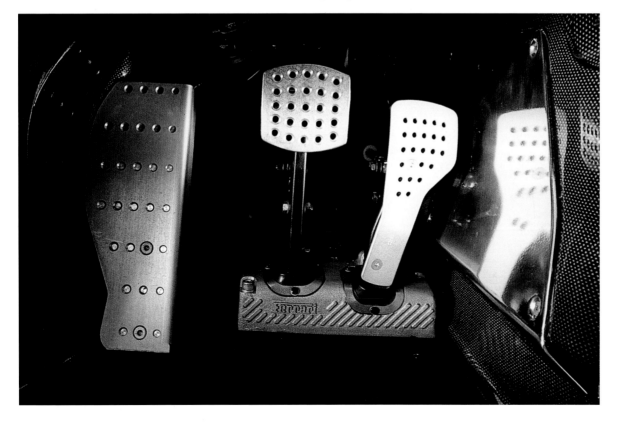

Wall Street Journal. In other publications, Losee adds, "They quoted me saying some things I have no recollection of saying as far as how fast I thought I was going. They say I said I was going around 150 mph… I don't remember saying that.

"The Highway Patrol showed up at my house 2–3 weeks later to collect on the ticket for the benefit. Plus, I had pledged another sum of money to their cause as well because, of course, I was in the hospital at the end of the event in Salt Lake City when they had their charity auction.

"When they gave me the ticket they said they would have 'gone to court' and declared that I was doing at least 206 mph just prior to the accident, according to their investigation."

The Highway Patrol report explained: "(Losee) encountered several swells in the roadway and his car became airborne. When the car again contacted the road, the frame struck the ground. The car began to slide to its right side and completed a 360-degree rotation and it left the road to the left. It then struck an embankment and was vaulted into the air. It flew a considerable distance and then landed. The engine and transmission as well as several other components became separated from the car as it began tumbling along the side of the road. The car then slid across the highway while upside down and after leaving the road to the right it tipped back on its wheels just as it came to a rest."

Says Losee: "At that speed I was pretty much a passenger. The fantastic Ferrari Enzo held together and did what it was supposed to do, which was to shed various and sundry parts on the way to keeping the occupant

An Enzo's interior is like a fantasy land of carbon fiber, leather, and exquisite detailing. There are switchable-menu instrument readouts, steering wheel levers for shifting the gearbox, and that most important of all controls, a big red Start button for the V-12 that is just behind the cockpit.

❖ *"At that speed I was pretty much a passenger.* The carbon
fiber capsule kept me alive. The full-face helmet certainly contributed and then
came Lieutenant Anderson, who had the courage and experience to get me
breathing."* — Richard Losee

alive. The carbon fiber capsule kept me alive.
The full-face helmet certainly contributed
and then came Lieutenant Anderson, who
had the courage and experience to get me
breathing."

Did the high-speed crash with the Enzo
sour Losee on Ferrari? Hardly.

"I have loved Ferraris since I first knew
about them. My dad had his first one in the
1960s. I don't feel any differently now than I
did. In fact, I'm really grateful that the car was
engineered and built as well as it was, because
if it wasn't we wouldn't be speaking now."

Ferrari Enzo S/N 131320 remains in
hundreds of pieces and will likely never be
rebuilt. Losee has considered replacing the
wrecked Enzo with another, but adds, "I don't
know about getting another Enzo… we did a
lot of special things with that car… and I
have a 599 GTB coming."

A religious man, Losee has wondered
about his crash at 206 mph in the Enzo and
says, "I'm not a person who believes that
everything in life has a reason. I believe that
sometimes we're allowed to go out there
and use our agency and things happen
because we're human. Otherwise, how do
you explain the 2-year-old little girl who gets
run over in a driveway by a parent? Or that a
child in South Africa is born HIV positive?

"It's not really fair and I believe that in the
end it will all be worked out. However, I
don't think that was my time. I do think there
is divine intervention at times and I do think
prayers make a lot of difference. I don't know
why I was spared, but I don't think it was luck
that I'm still alive… and I'm still searching." ▣

**The Enzo's brochure is packed with 29
plates that have descriptions in Italian
and English, and are accompanied by a
CD with duplicates of the images.**

Challenge Stradale was the name Ferrari gave to this lightweight version of the 360 Modena. Added use of carbon fiber, titanium, aluminum, and a Lexan rear window shave some 250 pounds from the standard 360. Titanium springs are part of a suspension package that is stiffer and drops the ride height by a half inch. Behind the wheels are advanced carbon ceramic brakes. With the 3.6-liter V-8's power increased by 25 horsepower to 425, the Stradale's 0–60 mph time is down around 4.0 seconds.

Ferrari replaced the 456 GT 2+2 with the 612 Scaglietti, the latter honoring long-time body maker Sergio Scaglietti. Here it is parked in front of the door to Enzo Ferrari's office at Ferrari's Fiorano test track. Pininfarina's shape for the 612 has historic overtones, including the egg-crate grille and side sculpting seen on a famous 375 MM owned by actress Ingrid Bergman's husband, director Roberto Rossellini. This is Ferrari's first V-12 automobile to have both its external sheetmetal and space-frame chassis made of weight-saving aluminum. The 5.7-liter V-12 boasts 540 horsepower and can be matched to a 6-speed manual or paddle-shifted electro-hydraulic semi-automatic transmission. The 612 hits a top speed just shy of 200 mph, and it reaches 60 mph in 4.6 seconds.

• 612 Scaglietti in China

Above: Ferrari's 612 Scaglietti drawing a crowd in rural China. Below: Patrick Hong driving the Ferrari 612 past Lhasa, Tibet's Potola Palace.

WE WERE PRIMED FOR DRAMA AND DEPRIVATION. SNOWY MOUNTAIN PASSES. LEAPING BEARDED GOATS, grizzled Tibetan mountain men and, with luck, a yeti. Freezing winds, bitter cold, and certainly nausea and debilitating headaches because we'd be in the thin air at 17,457 feet on the highest paved road in the world.

Sounds like fun, doesn't it?

The drive was part of Ferrari's "15,000 Red Miles," a tour throughout China to spread the automaker's name into that quickly expanding market and prove the reliability of its automobiles.

Our ride was a Ferrari 612 Scaglietti 2+2 that was only lightly modified to allow for rough roads, the altitude, and the possibility of low-grade fuel.

Ferrari's team had started in Shanghai, aimed north to Beijing, and from there was basically driving to the four corners of that huge country. Patrick Hong and I from *Road & Track* picked up the 1400-mile segment that would take us over the "top of the world" highway to Lhasa, Tibet.

Our entourage consisted of two 612s, a pair each of Fiat Palio wagons and IVECO trucks (for spares and luggage), an IVECO military-style vehicle in case of serious road troubles, and an SUV with a government guide.

We picked up our portion of the drive in the modern city of Lanzhou, some 450 miles southwest of Beijing, one day to Chaka, then to Golmud for three days acclimating to the 10,000-plus foot altitude before two days driving still higher country to Lhasa, Tibet.

The topography varied from the sort of green tall hills common in the western U.S. to vast stretches of desert to the broad valleys of the Tibetan Plateau. It was quite beautiful and thankfully devoid of billboards.

We passed through a few small cities, but generally the people we met were in tiny villages or nomads who live in tents—some highly decorated—and tend herds of yak and sheep.

For the most part, the roads were quite good, but we had to be alert. Suddenly the radio would bark, "SLOW, SLOW, *PIANO, PIANO!*" the lead Palio jinking hard right or left. There, after miles of smooth road would be a tire-bursting pothole. A few times we came across dreadful, several-kilometer stretches, obviously paving jobs given to someone's lazy brother-in-law. And after that it will be excellent for another 20 miles.

Traffic was light and consisted mainly of heavily laden, well-used tracks, locals on motorcycles, and an occasional new, highly polished SUV being driven quickly. Being a trucker on the road to Lhasa has to be one of the toughest driving jobs in the world, particularly in foul weather.

We came across a robed monk making the pilgrimage to Lhasa. Along the roadside he would prostrate himself, get up, take a step, prostrate himself again. . . actions he would repeat all the way to Lhasa, some 700 miles away. Whether you are religious or not, you have to admire his dedication.

We climbed the Tibetan Plateau, the largest in the world and source of 10 major rivers, including the Yellow, Yangtze and Mekong. This is when Patrick and I assumed we'd round a bend and begin The Big Climb up the highest paved road in the world.

It never happened.

Instead we gradually ascended the plateau along broad, beautiful valleys rimmed by the sort of snow-topped peaks we expected to cross but never approached.

And then, with little drama, we were there. We found two impressive statues and a pair of the Buddhist tent-like shrines made of long strips of cloth. In the background were tents for people hawking souvenirs. A stone marker affirmed we were at 5321 meters (17,457 feet) on the Tanggulashan Pass. . . and that was it.

Mind you, it was quite beautiful. Across the valley was another rank of snowy mountains. The air, though thin, couldn't have been fresher. And the sky was extraordinary. At this altitude, the clouds seem almost touchable and contrast strongly with the blue, which is deeper than at lower climes.

Lhasa was as impressive as predicted, the famous Potala Palace its centerpiece. Stick with the old section of this rapidly growing metropolis and you get a feeling for Lhasa as

it was. Narrow street markets, rickshaws competing with taxis, shops selling Himalayan trekking equipment and Buddhist artifacts. And there are the ever-present robed monks.

Ferrari's 15,000 Red Miles wasn't an easy journey, but it was worth every mile and moment and, by the way, the 612s never missed a beat. ▣

Below: **Road & Track's** *Patrick Hong at* **17,457** *feet on the highest paved road in the world with a Ferrari 612 Scaglietti.* *Bottom: The Italian 2+2 ran flawlessly on the* **1400** *miles of backcountry Chinese roads on which* **R&T** *drove it, ending up in Lhasa, Tibet.*

One of the world's great all-around exotic cars, Ferrari's F 430 is built as a coupe or spider. As with all modern Ferraris, both the space-frame chassis and bodywork of the F 430s are done in aluminum, which cuts weight without giving up structural stiffness. The 4.3-liter V-8 in this mid-engine sports car has 490 horsepower and, via a 6-speed manual or semi-automatic gearbox, will get the Ferrari to 60 mph in 3.5 seconds. Top speed is just over 190 mph.

The F 430 Spider's top is electrically operated and opens or closes in just 20 seconds.

Above: Ferrari's F 430 has numerous features that reflect the company's racing program. The steering wheel has the "START" button on left and the manettino on the right. This switch allows the driver to vary such settings as suspension firmness, transmission shifting, and throttle response. Below: The optional carbon-ceramic brakes have a much higher resistance to heat and fade, so you can use them with no fear of performance degradation (though they will degrade your wallet).

Previous pages: A rear three-quarter view of the 599 GTB Fiorano. Above: The 599 GTB Fiorano at the test track for which it is named, next to a display Formula 1 car. Inside, the main theme is leather with detailing in carbon fiber and aluminum. The tachometer can be had with a yellow or red background. Just ahead of the steering wheel are the shift paddles, while on the wheel's lower right is the manettino, the switch that allows the driver to alter several of the Ferrari's systems.

• Roberto Vaglietti

Head of Ferrari Classiche
Maranello, Italy

IF YOU OWN A FERRARI OF ANY VINTAGE AND WANT TO KNOW ANYTHING ABOUT THE HISTORY OF YOUR car, Roberto Vaglietti is the keeper of the keys.

As the head of Ferrari's Classiche department, his office is just steps away from the archives that house, among its thousands of documents, the build sheets for every car assembled in Maranello. A few steps further and you're in the huge, immaculate garage in which vintage Ferraris are restored by the factory. . . Berlinetta Boxers, 275 GTBs, Testa Rossas. . . you name it.

It's no accident Vaglietti works at Ferrari, but something he planned decades ago.

"I grew up in Switzerland," he begins, "and at the age of 11 Ferraris became something very important for me. Something of great significance." It probably didn't hurt that the first Ferrari that Vaglietti saw was a 250 GTO, the sort of automobile that could change a person's life.

"My aim was to one day work for the company. I decided to write directly to Enzo Ferrari to explain this dream and ask what could be done to achieve it. After a month or so, Mr. Ferrari wrote and said, 'Okay, but you are too young and have to continue to study, and one day when you have done this we will try to find a solution.'

"As a souvenir, he sent me a small book, which I have kept to this day. He also sent the job application form used by the factory then—this was 1961—and I kept that too." Vaglietti smiles and recalls, "I decided I would use it on that famous day when I was ready to work for Ferrari.

"I continued to contact Mr. Ferrari. When Ferrari race cars won I would write to him about the good result. He would write back to me. Just a few words, of course, but always encouraging me."

✦ *"After 3 years of technical school,* the opportunity came to join Ferrari, which I did by using the job application Mr. Ferrari sent to me when I was 11." — *Roberto Vaglietti*

When only 16 years old, "I decided to move to Italy and pursue my dream of working for Ferrari. In Maranello they had established the technical school named for Dino Ferrari, and I thought, 'What a good opportunity.' I started my studies there in October 1966.

"I was living with a family in Maranello," he continues, "and the father worked at Ferrari. On some occasions, such as Christmas, I could join the parties Enzo Ferrari would have for the children of his employees. I had a chance to talk with him for the first time at Christmas, 1966. I told him, 'I am very happy to know you, my name is Vaglietti.' He said, 'Ah, you are the young Swiss writing to me.' The fact he remembered my name was unforgettable.

"After 3 years of technical school, the opportunity came to join Ferrari, which I did by using the job application Mr. Ferrari sent to me when I was 11. They asked, 'Where did you get this form?' and I told them I got

it in 1961, directly from Enzo Ferrari. And that's how my career at Ferrari began."

Vaglietti had to move back to Switzerland for two years and worked for Filipinetti, the Ferrari importer, but returned to Italy in January 1971 and finally had his job at Ferrari in Maranello. "My dream was to become involved in the driving at Ferrari, and I started as a production test driver. I was only 20 and I had my dream job."

How many young men around the world have had that dream? And what happened?

"Unfortunately, after two months I had a severe accident (in a Fiat Dino), which is the only one I have had... touch wood." Vaglietti thought his job at Ferrari was over, but they kept him on. A few months later, the just-turned-21 driver moved up to testing Daytonas and Dino 246s. Vaglietti still recalls his first test Ferrari: a blue Daytona.

And now he's the man in charge of knowing just when those Daytonas and Dinos and any other car made by Ferrari were built. 🅵

Ferrari's Classiche department has the build records of every car made in Maranello. Located at the factory, it also does restorations, such as the one taking place with the 275 GTB at left or, with a bit more effort, the Testa Rossa below.

• Patrick Hong on Testing Ferraris

Senior Techinical Editor, Road & Track
Irvine, California

Above, Patrick Hong drives the Enzo around the cones during the Road & Track road test.

HOW'S THIS FOR A DREAM JOB? YOU'RE A 25-YEAR-OLD GUY WHO LOVES FAST CARS AND YOU'VE GOT Ferrari's Fiorano test track to yourself, a brand new 360 Modena purring at idle.

Your mission? Find out just how fast the Ferrari will go, getting the numbers down to two places past the decimal point.

Patrick Hong arrived at Fiorano armed with plenty of experience testing cars for *Road & Track,* an engineer's methodical approach to working through any situation, and a Master's degree in aerodynamics from USC.

Hong recalls his first test on that most hallowed ground in Maranello: "It was like going to Mecca. Just being at Fiorano, Ferrari's office right there—it's something you never imagined you'd be able to do. And then to be testing the car. . . ."

Hong had driven an F 355—first of the "Montezemolo" cars—and knew it had been a giant step up from the 348. Now he'd test the 360 Modena, and get a taste of Italian style while doing runs up and down the main straightaway. "It's just over a quarter-mile down the straight so you have to brake hard at the first corner after the acceleration runs. I was doing quick turn-arounds and one time partially spun the car. There are apartments next to the track and a lady up in one of them was cheering for me.

"I also remember riding with Dario Benuzzi (Ferrari's legendary test driver) in the 360. He's going so quickly, sliding the car, steering with one finger, looking over at me, smiling. I happened to tape record the lap. When I played it back, all I could hear was the engine revving and me laughing."

A decade later, Hong, now 35, has tested or driven extensively all the modern Montezemolo Ferraris. He shows an understandable generational view as he begins with the 2+2 Ferraris.

"I did like the 456's styling—very distinctive—but it was a weird car for me, as I associate Ferrari with mid-engine sports cars.

"The 612 is a long, comfortable car, but too huge for me. They hide the size well and you can't really tell in photos, but when you're driving it, it's a long car.

"It is comfortable, even on the roads on which I drove it in China. And the V-12 has so much power you don't feel as though you are tasking it much. There is power whenever you need it, so it's a very relaxing sort of driving experience. No need to be on-the-boil all the time, and that's the beauty of V-12s.

"I suppose if I were older the 575 or 599 would be my choice. The 599 is fantastic car with all the performance of a boy racer, but more mature and with a more robust stance. I'm not certain I like the 599's styling as much as the F 430's, though I do like the design of the arch at the back of the Grand Touring car's greenhouse where the glass falls away— a nice touch.

"Driving-wise it has almost as much power as the Enzo, just tuned differently. I didn't test the car, but drove it on the Autostrada and into mountains in Italy. I think the 599 is what Montezemolo wanted to shoot for, no-nonsense reliability and quality, with an Italian flare.

"I still think an F 430 represents Ferrari more than does the 599. To some people

❖ **"I still think an F 430 represents Ferrari** *more than does the 599. To some people Ferrari means front-engine, rear-drive GT cars and that's what the 599 is, but I grew up on mid-engine exotics and that's what Ferrari means to me."* — Patrick Hong

Ferrari means front-engine, rear-drive GT cars and that's what the 599 is, but I grew up on mid-engine exotics and that's what Ferrari means to me.

"I think the F 355 coupe and convertible are terrific-looking cars. When driving the F 355 you have to pay more attention and in some ways that's good because you feel you are more involved, more of a boy racer, while the 360 doesn't have quite as much character.

"That's an important distinction with Ferraris. They are very fast—not always the fastest in the world—but at least when you drive them you feel like you are more involved in the process."

He also appreciates the technical side of modern Ferraris. "Everyone has upped the

On his first trip to Fiorano, Hong was given a typically quick ride by the factory's legendary chief test driver, Dario Benuzzi (below), here seen sliding the F 355. Hong recalls, "He was going so quickly, sliding the car, steering with one finger, just looking over at me, smiling."

game and Ferrari is as good as anyone out there. I think they are on the leading edge. They led in building aluminum chassis, and the 360 was probably the first application where engineers thought about how to make an aluminum car from scratch, as opposed to making a steel car out of aluminum, as Audi did."

Hong particularly likes the F 430, saying, "I would own the F 430 before most exotic cars in the world. It's a bit of a throwback to the F 355 compared to the 360 Modena, a bit more of a boy racer. The styling has more flare and I think the F 430 Spider is terrific. I think I would prefer the manual, even though I love the paddle shifter."

As for the argument of the F1 semi-automatic transmission versus the traditional manual gearbox: "The first F 355 I drove had a manual, gated shifter and I really didn't like it." When

the 360 came along with the paddle shifters I thought it was terrific. But afterwards I had the opportunity to drive the 575 Maranello and the 360 in one test and had a chance to work with the manual. Now I almost enjoy it a little better. I like hearing that metallic click as you shift from gear to gear. On a track I probably still prefer the paddles, but for day-to-day driving I prefer that click-click. You feel like you've accomplished something. It's that

❖ **"It was like going to Mecca. Just being at Fiorano,** *Ferrari's office right there... it's something you never imagined you'd be able to do... and then to be testing the car...."* — *Patrick Hong*

involvement thing again."

There's no greater involvement than in one of Hong's favorites: the Enzo. However, his first Ferrari supercar impressions really began with the F 40 because, "I grew up reading about it and was impressed back then. When I finally got in it, the car felt dated because it was then 15 years old, but it was great fun. A lot of things are happening and you feel like you're in a Ferrari race car."

And then came a rare opportunity to drive an Enzo for hundreds of miles, followed by a track test.

"What struck me about the Enzo was how it's fast but so stable. We were on a road in the middle of nowhere, a downhill then uphill stretch with a mile or two where I could see that there was no traffic and no intersecting roads. So I punched it and took the Enzo to 175 mph and it felt absolutely stable even at that speed. It felt like the car never changed—so little difference between 60 mph, 120 mph, and 175 mph.

"All this is because of active aerodynamics and ride height. It is amazing what the Enzo can do as a high-performance car and still be almost a daily driver—much more so than an F 40. It actually rides nicely, with good damping and it's not too harsh. I love the attention to details, like the exposed instrument panel, the ducting, the steering rack and shaft.

"The moment you sit in it, even before you start the engine, you know you're in something special because everything about that car looks so different. The SLR looks like a super-sized Mercedes SL, the Porsche Carrera GT and Bugatti Veyron are very nice inside, like luxury cars, but an Enzo is simply out of the ordinary, something special you don't see everyday." 🄵

Road & Track's *35-year-old Senior Technical Editor shows a generational bias when he prefers the mid-engine F 430 to the front-engine 599 GTB (left). But he also says, "The 599 is a fantastic car with all the performance of a boy racer, but more mature and with a more robust stance."*

Road & Track test results:

	550 M Maranello	599 GTB Fiorano	F 355 Coupe	360 Modena	F 430	Enzo
0-60 mph	4.7 sec	3.2 sec	4.9 sec	4.3 sec	3.5 sec	3.3 sec
0-100 mph	10.5 sec	7.0 sec	11.3 sec	10.2 sec	8.1 sec	6.6 sec
top speed*	199 mph	205 mph	183 mph	189 mph	198 mph	218 mph

* estimated

• **Frank Stephenson and the Pininfarina Show Cars**
Director of Design, Fiat Auto
Torino, Italy

THEY HAVE BEEN THE STUFF OF OUR AUTOMOTIVE DREAMS. WE LUSTED AFTER THEIR LINES, IMAGINED their power, and wondered what it would be like to once—just once—slip behind the steering wheel and blast down some lightly traveled road.

But all we could do was stare at them in awe, up there on the stand at an auto show or splashed across the pages of a magazine like *Road & Track*. Their entire purpose was to yank our chains… and it worked very nicely indeed.

But what should we call them?

Today they are known as concept cars and are a means for automakers to set a broad design theme for the future, to float an idea for a production machine, or to drum up sales interest for an upcoming production model.

It was different in Ferrari's early years when the specials were called show cars because that was their purpose: to display Ferrari's wares at famous auto shows in Paris, Geneva, Turin, Frankfurt, London, and New York.

The little enamel emblems on the bodies read like an honor roll of Italian carrozzeria: Vignale, Ghia, Stabilimenti Farina, Touring, Boano, Zagato, and Pinin Farina.

Frank Stephenson, the American who was Ferrari's GT Department Concept Design and Development Director and now heads design for Fiat, explains: "Ferrari had show cars early on because special customers (often royalty or famous movie stars) wanted special cars. In a sense, each of those cars was an advanced prototype, a show car made for the road. It was a strong point at Ferrari that they made one-off unique show cars that were runners."

As of the early 1960s, the vast majority of such show cars were done by Pininfarina, which had become (with the exception of Bertone's 308 GT4) the exclusive supplier of body design for Ferrari, a position it holds today. On rare occasions other carrozzeria such as Bertone would produce a Ferrari show car, likely with hopes of drumming up some business, but never to any avail.

As Ferrari got more serious about mass production in the mid-1960s the creation of show cars for individual buyers tapered off. Pininfarina made the swing to what we now call concept cars, creating a series of wonderful machines that pointed the direction for the upcoming Dino series, while the 1969 P6 hinted at the Boxer.

And for a few years Pininfarina produced a handful of Ferraris that were among the most exciting show automobiles created. It began with the 1968 250 P5 Berlinetta Speciale, followed the next year by the 512 S. And then, in 1970, the car that blew us all away, the 512 S Modulo.

It's one of Stephenson's favorites. "As a kid I had that Matchbox model for the longest time and didn't even know it was a Ferrari, but just loved to look at the car. It just looked like something that landed from outer space."

There were other great Ferrari concepts from Pininfarina—the 1974 CR 25 aerodynamic study and the 1980 Pinin, an elegant suggestion for a 4-door Ferrari—but the next true heartbreaker Ferrari show car from Pininfarina was the 1989 Mythos, a shape that so charmed several men they had

the carrozzeria build copies for their own use. How's that for exclusive?

There are still plenty of show—make that concept—cars today, but fewer with Ferrari underpinnings. Pininfarina did show the Rosso. "[The Rosso] showed almost Formula 1 influence on a GT body," Stephenson explains. "That's an important point at Ferrari, the fact it has such a strong F1 link and whatever you bring over from that side is, for me, the Ferrari of today."

Others might suggest that while there aren't as many one-off Ferrari show cars as there once was, they now do models that are just as special, but in large batches, like the 400 Enzos Ferrari says it built.

Good point, but the thought of an all-new one-off Ferrari show car is enough to make Stephenson grin.

"That would be the ultimate job for a car designer: do a Ferrari show car, something really far out, a Ferrari for 15 years from now." F

Although most concept cars are built as one-offs, Pininfarina has made duplicates of some of its show machines for private collections. Shiro Kosaka's Abarth Gallery in Yamanashi, Japan has a 1989 Ferrari Mythos by Pininfarina.

Grand Prix

GRAND PRIX
The Dynasty

Previous pages: Michael Schumacher wails though the water on his way to winning the 2004 Japanese Grand Prix in a Ferrari F 2004. Below: The line-up of factory- and privately-owned Formula 1 Ferraris at the 2004 Rolex Monterey Historic Automobile Races.

ANYONE WHO HAS EVEN A PASSING INTEREST IN AUTOMOBILE RACING KNOWS what happened with Ferrari Grand Prix racing in the first five years of the new century… five World Championships for Michael Schumacher and five constructors' titles for Ferrari. In the best year, 2004, Schumacher won 12 of the 13 first races.

Even in 2005 and 2006 when Fernando Alonso and Renault took both titles, Schumacher was beating on the door, and his teammates—Rubens Barrichello in 2005, Felipe Massa in 2006—were generally right in the hunt. **F**

Showing their typical enthusiasm, Scuderia Ferrari team manager Jean Todt (left) and drivers Rubens Barrichello (center) and Michael Schumacher celebrate after the 2003 Japanese Grand Prix. Barrichello had just won the race. Although Schumacher finished only eighth, he wrapped up that year's Formula 1 driver's championship. This was his sixth title, eclipsing the record of the great Juan Manuel Fangio. The German driver would go on to win his seventh crown—again with Ferrari—in 2004.

Ferrari has developed a clientele service for those who would like to purchase one of the Scuderia's older Formula 1 cars. The factory not only makes the cars available, but also offers full service for the F1 machines, which is important because they are highly sophisticated devices. Left: Californian Jim Busby leaves the garage at Fiorano in his 1996 Ferrari during a test session. Above: Tony Noble, also from California, on the track in his 2001 Formula 1 Ferrari. Noble's car is the one in which Michael Schumacher won the Belgian Grand Prix in 2001 to become the winningest driver in Grand Prix history. This is also the car that raced with no signage and a black nosecone in the 2001 Italian Grand Prix—and then again with American flags at the United States Grand Prix—to honor the victims of the 9/11 terrorist attacks.

• **Luca Cordero di Montezemolo**

Chairman, Ferrari S.p.A.
Maranello, Italy

LUCA DI MONTEZEMOLO HAS ALWAYS BEEN WILLING TO SPEAK HIS MIND. HE WAS THE NEWLY APPOINTED assistant to Enzo Ferrari when he attended the British Grand Prix in July 1973, a year when the automaker's Formula 1 fortunes were dim. He told the press, "It would have been better for Ferrari not to have come at all than with cars like this."

Six month later Montezemolo was put in charge of the F1 team, which went on to win the series' constructors' championship in 1975, 1976, and 1977. Like Enzo Ferrari, Luca di Montezemolo can inspire men to do great things.

During 1977, Montezemolo moved to the corporate side of Fiat, Ferrari's parent company. He began a succession of posts that included everything from heading public relations to overseeing Fiat's printing subsidiary to running Cinzano—the famous Italian vermouth company—to the sports side, organizing Italy's America's Cup entry and the world soccer finals.

Quite a varied career, but when Ferrari fell into difficult times after the death of Enzo Ferrari, Montezemolo was asked to return to the automaker and fix it.

Which he did in spades, the company revamping its production cars into a series of best sellers and putting its Grand Prix team back at the front of the grid.

A decade and a half after returning to Ferrari, Montezemolo points out that they made the transition, "Without a change of history, a change of spirit, and without losing the core business of our tradition, because every single Ferrari model has a small but important link with the past."

How did the plan succeed so well?

"I think basically by putting our people, our products, and our clients at the center of our activities. Making cars that are innovative and unique, maintaining exclusivity, and engineering cars you can enjoy everyday and not just as a sunny Sunday car." Montezemolo points to this quality as being a major reason behind the success of the new 599 Fiorano, which has a two-year waiting list of orders.

Montezemolo is big believer in taking care of his own, of paying, "A lot of attention to the people, to the organization, and to the motivation. Ferrari has to remain the best place to work in Europe. Twice we won that prize from the *Financial Times*.

"For me this has been as unique as six world constructors' championship titles running against the most important car manufacturers in the world, because now Formula 1 is a competition between Toyota, Renault, BMW, Honda, and Mercedes, not like in the 1970s or 1980s with the English, shall I say, assembly guys.

"So we must maintain the same passion, same exclusivity, same challenge, and same

innovation spirit without losing the link to the past. . . looking ahead and opening windows to our suppliers and to the world."

Along the way, Ferrari's factory in Maranello has been transformed into an industrial showplace. Not only does Ferrari have the most up-to-date equipment, but it is housed in buildings that are statements of not only the architectural art, but also worker- and ecology-friendly environments.

The one thing that hasn't changed? The traditional gateway to the factory, "Which I will keep as it was forever. . . ."

Montezemolo maintains that, "Maranello is still a village, it's still Maranello, it's not New York or Rome, and so our link with the territory remains very strong."

Then he adds, "We have improved quality and the high tech approach because. . . when I arrived in Ferrari I felt I didn't want us to become *The Last of The Mohicans*. Like Greta Garbo, an aging actress without any scripts. I want us to be Ferrari, but looking ahead.

"If you enter a Ferrari you still have the same emotion, a car made in a small village and done inside the company by fantastic people." **F**

Above: Maranello has been transformed into a modern industrial showplace. Shown is the Ferrari/Alcoa facility responsible for the all-aluminum chassis and bodies. Below: The automated engine-machining factory.

❖ *"Maranello is still a village, it's still Maranello,* it's not New York or Rome, and so our link with the territory remains very strong."
— *Luca di Montezemolo*

Ferrari's super Enzo, the FXX. Maranello built 32 of these semi-competition machines, which cost $2 million and are not meant for the street, but special Ferrari track events. While the V-12 engine is based on the Enzo's, its displacement is 6.3 liters and horsepower comes in at 790. The gear-box, brakes and suspension have been upgraded to match the power, and the FXX rides on 19-inch slick tires.

Index